THE WAY
PEOPLE
LIVE

Life
Among the Vikings

Titles in The Way People Live series include:

THE WAY PEOPLE LIVE

Life Among the Vikings

by Thomas Streissguth

Lucent Books, P.O. Box 289011, San Diego, CA 92198-9011

Library of Congress Cataloging-in-Publication Data

Streissguth, Thomas, 1958–
   Life among the Vikings / by Thomas Streissguth.
      p.   cm. — (The way people live)
   Includes bibliographical references and index.
   Summary: Discusses the history, settlements, social structure, religion, occupations, and culture of the Vikings.
   ISBN 1-56006-392-0 (lib. : alk. paper)
   1. Vikings—Civilization—Juvenile literature.   [1. Vikings.]   I. Title.
II. Series.
DL65.S86   1999
948'.022—dc21   98-30344
                                                                          CIP
                                                                           AC

Copyright 1999 by Lucent Books, Inc., P.O. Box 289011, San Diego, California 92198-9011

Printed in the U.S.A.

Contents

Discovering the Humanity in Us All

Books in The Way People Live series focus on groups of people in a wide variety of circumstances, settings, and time periods. Some books focus on different cultural groups, others, on people in a particular historical time period, while others cover people involved in a specific event. Each book emphasizes the daily routines, personal and historical struggles, and achievements of people from all walks of life.

To really understand any culture, it is necessary to strip the mind of the common notions we hold about groups of people. These stereotypes are the archenemies of learning. It does not even matter whether the stereotypes are positive or negative; they are confining and tight. Removing them is a challenge that's not easily met, as anyone who has ever tried it will admit. Ideas that do not fit into the templates we create are unwelcome visitors—ones we would prefer remain quietly in a corner or forgotten room.

The cowboy of the Old West is a good example of such confining roles. The cowboy was courageous, yet soft-spoken. His time (it is always a he, in our template) was spent alternatively saving a rancher's daughter from certain death on a runaway stagecoach, or shooting it out with rustlers. At times, of course, he was likely to get a little crazy in town after a trail drive, but for the most part, he was the epitome of inner strength. It is disconcerting to find out that the cowboy is human, even a bit childish. Can it really be true that cowboys would line up to help the

cook on the trail drive grind coffee, just hoping he would give them a little stick of peppermint candy that came with the coffee shipment? The idea of tough cowboys vying with one another to help "Coosie" (as they called their cooks) for a bit of candy seems silly and out of place.

So is the vision of Eskimos playing video games and watching MTV, living in prefab housing in the Arctic. It just does not fit with what "Eskimo" means. We are far more comfortable with snow igloos and whale blubber, harpoons and kayaks.

Although the cultures dealt with in Lucent's The Way People Live series are often historically and socially well known, the emphasis is on the personal aspects of life. Groups of people, while unquestionably affected by their politics and their governmental structures, are more than those institutions. How do people in a particular time and place educate their children? What do they eat? And how do they build their houses? What kinds of work do they do? What kinds of games do they enjoy? The answers to these questions bring these cultures to life. People's lives are revealed in the particulars and only by knowing the particulars can we understand these cultures' will to survive and their moments of weakness and greatness.

This is not to say that understanding politics does not help to understand a culture. There is no question that the Warsaw ghetto, for example, was a culture that was brought about by the politics and social ideas of Adolf

Hitler and the Third Reich. But the Jews who were crowded together in the ghetto cannot be understood by the Reich's politics. Their life was a day-to-day battle for existence, and the creativity and methods they used to prolong their lives is a vital story of human perseverance that would be denied by focusing only on the institutions of Hitler's Germany. Knowing that children as young as five or six outwitted Nazi guards on a daily basis, that Jewish policemen helped the Germans control the ghetto, that children attended secret schools in the ghetto and even earned diplomas—these are the things that reveal the fabric of life, that can inspire, intrigue, and amaze.

Books in The Way People Live series allow both the casual reader and the student to see humans as victims, heroes, and onlookers. And although humans act in ways that can fill us with feelings of sorrow and revulsion, it is important to remember that "hero," "predator," and "victim" are dangerous terms. Heaping undue pity or praise on people reduces them to objects, and strips them of their humanity.

Seeing the Jews of Warsaw only as victims is to deny their humanity. Seeing them only as they appear in surviving photos, staring at the camera with infinite sadness, is limiting, both to them and to those who want to understand them. To an object of pity, the only appropriate response becomes "Those poor creatures!" and that reduces both the quality of their struggle and the depth of their despair. No one is served by such two-dimensional views of people and their cultures.

With this in mind, The Way People Live series strives to flesh out the traditional, two-dimensional views of people in various cultures and historical circumstances. Using a wide variety of primary quotations—the words not only of the politicians and government leaders, but of the real people whose lives are being examined—each book in the series attempts to show an honest and complete picture of a culture removed from our own by time or space.

By examining cultures in this way, the reader will notice not only the glaring differences from his or her own culture, but also will be struck by the similarities. For indeed, people share common needs—warmth, good company, stability, and affirmation from others. Ultimately, seeing how people really live, or have lived, can only enrich our understanding of ourselves.

The Vikings: Legend and Reality

For three hundred years, the people of the British Isles, Europe, and the Mediterranean basin feared no enemy as much as they feared the Vikings. These Scandinavian pagans attacked cities and settlements throughout the Western world. The armies of England and France could not cope with them; the emperor of mighty Byzantium could not stop their raids on his wealthy capital city of Constantinople. The Vikings harried Saxony, Moorish Spain, the city-states of Italy, and the islands of Greece. They burned, looted, murdered, and kidnapped. They stole money and valuables, and they ransomed their captives, and sometimes even entire countries, for enormous fortunes in silver.

But all that took place at least nine centuries ago. By now, the Viking legends have long replaced reality. The Vikings are a myth, not a threat, and the people of Scandinavia see them as heroic ancestors. They honor the Vikings in museums, in art and movies, at archaeological sites, and during gatherings that imitate Viking life and society. This view of the Vikings began as the Scandinavian peoples were asserting themselves as nations of equal standing to the kingdoms of Europe. The Icelandic sagas—long prose poems that provided the raw material of poetry and legends—arrived on the scene just as the Vikings had: by sea. As historian Eric Oxenstierna reports, "Sailing vessels came from Iceland, bringing parchment volumes that had been handed down from generation to generation and read on that island. They told of heroic deeds of the

pagan ancestor; of pride, honor and valorous military expeditions in foreign lands."[1] Scandinavian rulers of the sixteenth century and beyond saw in their armies the legacy of Viking strength and heroics. The Viking myth became a source of national pride that exists to this day.

Vikings in the Modern Mind

When people in the rest of the world imagine the Vikings, they may have only half a picture—the half that was painted by the enemies and victims of the Vikings. They may see slender wooden ships gliding along the rivers and coasts of Europe, with crews of bloodthirsty pagans wearing horned helmets and brandishing swords, axes, and spears. They may not think of Viking traders, artisans, farmers, and families. They may have only a vague notion of the Viking religion and the runic alphabet that the Vikings used to inscribe stones, weapons, and monuments. They may have no notion at all of how the Vikings dressed themselves, prepared their food, carried out overseas trade, raised crops, or furnished their homes.

The vague and often false images of the Vikings exist because the Scandinavians of this era left behind very little information about themselves. They kept no diaries and wrote no history books. They left only picture stones—short inscriptions written in runes—a few lines of poetry, and the scattered re-

Commonly held notions about Vikings are often romanticized and inaccurate. What little information modern scholars possess about these raiders comes from the remains of picture stones, cities, and graves.

mains of Viking homes, cities, and graves. The only remaining firsthand accounts were left by their victims and enemies: the Christians of Europe and the Muslims of the Middle East, who saw the Vikings, as many people still do, solely as raiders and pagans.

As a result, historians and archaeologists have been wondering, guessing, and arguing about Viking society for centuries. To fill the gaps in their knowledge, these experts rely on their own intuition—accurate or inaccurate—about their subject. As historian P. H. Sawyer notes,

> The only evidence available to check and test the written sources is that provided by the auxiliary studies . . . the evidence of place-names, archaeology and numismatics [the study of coins]. Archaeological discoveries, place-names and coins them-

selves have no bias, they do not yield a Scandinavian point of view. The bias is imposed by those working with the material. And here lies the great difficulty for the historian who seeks a more balanced view of the Viking period.[2]

Each new book by a Viking historian puts forward new theories in an attempt to explain the scanty evidence. Each writer has his or her own idea about the silent clues left behind by the Vikings themselves: coins, weapons, jewelry, foundations, buried ships, and graves. Many questions and puzzles still remain, making the Viking era an exciting, ever-changing field of study in which some questions may never be answered. However, historians using guesswork, imagination, and archaeological evidence continue to piece together what they know of life among the Vikings.

1

The Viking Encounter

On a late spring day in the year 789, three long and slender ships appeared on the horizon off the coast of Dorset in the Anglo-Saxon kingdom of Wessex. The visitors lowered their large, rectangular mainsails and swiftly rowed their ships into the harbor of the town of Portland. Those on shore who first sighted the ships may have believed them to be carrying traders from northern Europe who came to peacefully barter goods. These observers would have been mistaken.

The anonymous author of the *Anglo-Saxon Chronicle* describes what happened next:

789 . . . there came for the first time three ships of Northmen, and then the reeve [agent of the king] rode to them and wished to force them to the king's residence, for he did not know what they were, and they slew him. Those were the first ships of Danish men which came to the land of the English.[3]

A group of Danish raiders preparing to set sail for England. The Vikings first appear in English records in the late eighth century.

The reeve, whose name was Aethelweard, had served as a minister of King Beorhtric of Wessex. He and his small company of men would be the first Britons to die at the hands of the troublesome Scandinavian raiders known today as the Vikings.

Island Sanctuaries

Beorhtric, Aethelweard, and the people of the small Anglo-Saxon kingdoms of Britain were not prepared for the Vikings. Absorbed in their own civil conflicts and rivalries, they had not experienced foreign wars or invasions in many years. Norwegians and Danes had been rare visitors, primarily as traders who brought fur pelts, amber, and other articles from the north to exchange for English goods—clothing, salt, weapons—that were scarce in their own homelands. Scandinavia itself was almost unknown to even the most knowledgeable English chroniclers, monks, and geographers. It lay safely distant across the turbulent North Sea, in a cold part of the world inhabited only by mythical beasts and scattered settlements of violent, uncivilized pagans.

For these reasons, there were no fortifications or navies protecting the coasts of Britain or Ireland. The islands that dotted the bays and seas of the British Isles were also unprotected. Many of these islands served as peaceful sanctuaries for Christian monks who sought escape from civil strife on the mainland. Hundreds of tiny communities of fishermen, hermits, sheperds, and sailors lived open to the sea and vulnerable to everything the sea might bring.

One of these quiet island sanctuaries, Lindisfarne, lay just off the coast of Northumbria in northeastern England. Lindisfarne was home to an order of Irish monks whose

What's in a Viking Name?

As the Danish Vikings conquered new land and began settling in northeastern England (the Danelaw), they brought their language to the land of the Anglo-Saxons. Many Old Norse words made their way into the English language; some have survived in the dialects of Yorkshire and Lincolnshire, where *bairn* means child, *toft* means farmhouse, and *lathe* means barn. Many place names also show the legacy of the Danish invasion. Yorkshire itself, which was once part of the Danelaw, is now divided into East, West, and North Riding; the word *riding* comes from an Old Norse word that means "one-third part."

Other place names offer clues about the history of particular sites in this part of eastern Britain. Place names which end in *-ton* or *-tun* have combined a Norse name with the Old English suffix meaning "village." These places were renamed by the conquering Danes. Others end in *-by*, which is the Norse word that carries the same meaning as *-ton* or *-tun* in Old English. Those places that end in *-by*, such as the towns of Skewsby or Dalby or the small North Sea port town of Whitby, were actually founded by Danish settlers, perhaps on unoccupied land. The Norse suffix *-thorp* means a smaller settlement or a distant tract of land. Ganthorpe and Easthorpe were distant or smaller villages taken over by the Danes in later years, after the better land and farms were already occupied.

treasury held an array of valuable holy objects: manuscript books, gold and silver plates, goblets, reliquaries, crucifixes. The Lindisfarne treasury was unprotected by walls or earthworks; the monks were unarmed and unprepared. Directly east lay the

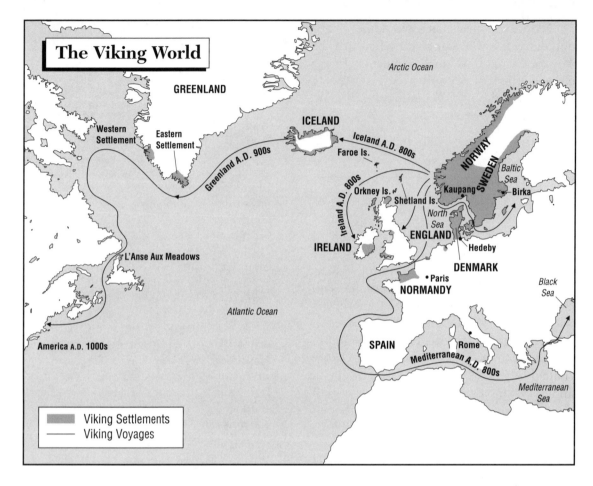

The Viking World

GREENLAND

Western Settlement

Eastern Settlement

Arctic Ocean

ICELAND

Iceland A.D. 800s

Faroe Is.

Greenland A.D. 900s

Ireland A.D. 800s

Orkney Is.

Shetland Is.

NORWAY

SWEDEN

Kaupang

Baltic Sea

Birka

North Sea

ENGLAND

L'Anse Aux Meadows

IRELAND

Hedeby

DENMARK

Atlantic Ocean

America A.D. 1000s

Paris

NORMANDY

Black Sea

SPAIN

Rome

Mediterranean A.D. 800s

Mediterranean Sea

■ Viking Settlements
— Viking Voyages

steep inlets and fjords of Norway, where the next party of Viking raiders set off in search of easy plunder.

Death on Lindisfarne

The raid on Lindisfarne took place on June 8, 793. The Vikings again had sailed in the late spring, in fair weather. Guided by the stars, the sun and moon, the flights of birds, and even the patterns of waves in the sea, they navigated several hundred miles southwest from Norway without the aid of landmarks of any kind. As they approached the island, they lowered their sails, began rowing the oars that

emerged from both sides of their boats, and prepared their long-bladed iron swords, stout axes, and daggers.

The Vikings did not need a sheltered port—the shallow keels of their ships allowed them to simply run their vessels up onto Lindisfarne's flat beach. The raiders leapt from the boats and rushed to the church of St. Cuthbert, dedicated to the island's protective saint. Monks who were unable or unwilling to flee the island were murdered. The invaders slaughtered sheep and cattle, then feasted in the burning ruins of the church and monastery buildings. They stayed for several weeks, gathering chests of heavy loot before returning home to celebrate their triumph.

News of the raid on Lindisfarne spread quickly, setting off a wave of terror in England as well as the European continent. The English chronicler Alcuin, who was living at the court of the Frankish king Charlemagne, wrote, "We and our forefathers have lived here for about 350 years, and never have such terrors as these appeared in Britain, which we must now suffer from the pagans; it was not thought possible that such havoc could be made."[4]

Divine Punishment

Unable to account for the sudden violence that had arrived on the coasts of Britain, the people and their leaders searched the heavens for telltale signs. Natural portents served as warnings for such disasters, and in the year of the Lindisfarne raid, states *The Anglo-Saxon Chronicle*, "immense whirlwinds and flashes of lightning, and fiery dragons were seen flying in the air. . . . A little after that in the same year, on June 8, the ravages of heathen men miserably destroyed God's church on Lindisfarne."[5]

The raids continued, year after year. Believing the raids signified divine punishment for their sins, the Christians of Britain prayed for deliverance from the pagans. The island of Jarrow was attacked in 794, and the islands of Saint Patrick and Columban in the Irish Sea were hit the next year. Viking ships landed on the rocky islands and the rugged coast of Scotland in the late 790s and early 800s. Each spring, as the weather turned fair and favorable winds blew from the east, the terrifying dragon-headed Viking ships appeared from Norway and Denmark on the eastern horizon.

The ships landed on islands laying offshore or along the banks of sheltered river estuaries. The Northmen, tall and sturdy, hurried to their intended targets before a defensive force could be assembled. They dressed in coarse wool tunics and wore helmets of leather or iron. They spoke the "Danish" tongue, as the English called it, and, on certain days, sacrificed animals and sometimes people to their pagan gods. They used their island camps as semipermanent bases

The British Isles were unprepared for the swift and devastating raids of the Norsemen. Because no one could predict when or where the Vikings would land, the victims often viewed the Vikings' arrival as a form of divine punishment.

for long seasons of burning, killing, and looting. At the end of the summer, when the prevailing winds shifted to the west and southwest, they sailed away.

Unfortunately for Britain and its islands, the Vikings sought land as well as loot. With fertile, level ground scarce in their Scandinavian homeland, the Vikings began seizing territory and building settlements. By the end of the eighth century, Norwegian Viking farmers had built small hamlets and fishing villages in the Shetland and Orkney Islands and off the northern coasts of Scotland. Vikings also settled the distant Hebrides and the Isle of Man, which lay between Great Britain and Ireland.

To Ireland and Frisia

By the year 800, Norwegian Vikings had also become regular and unwelcome visitors to Ireland, a rural land dotted with isolated monasteries. The Irish offered little resistance to the raiders, whose slender ships easily navigated the narrow streams leading inland from the sea. "The Ocean poured torrents of foreigners over Erin," states the *Annals of Erin,* "so that not a harbour or landing, fort or stronghold, was without fleets of Scandinavians and pirates."[6]

To take full advantage of this opportunity, the Vikings built a settlement on Lambay Island, near the mouth of the Liffey River in eastern Ireland. In 836 they moved to the mainland to build the town and port of Dublin. An embankment was built along the Liffey, and Dublin soon became a prospering trading port. Viking chiefs also founded the Irish towns of Limerick and Cork.

In 832 a large Norwegian fleet appeared along the Irish coast carrying a chief named Turges, who fought, raided, plundered, and extended his domain over half of Ireland. Turges finally proclaimed himself king of Ireland in 839 and turned the Christian shrine at Armagh into a pagan temple dedicated to the Norse god Thor. As historian Holger Arbman writes,

He called himself abbot of Armagh, and his wife chanted heathen spells on the cathedral's high altar. The chronicle [the *Annals of Erin*] accuses him of attempting to convert the whole island to the worship of Thor, but this is very unlikely. His death was followed by a rising against the Vikings, the standard figure for whose losses in a defeat in the Irish chronicles is 12,000.[7]

In 799 Danish Vikings sailed west to attack Frisia, the low-lying, sandy coast of what is now the Netherlands. To guard the northern shores of his Frankish kingdom, the em-

To protect the shores of his empire, Charlemagne organized seaborne patrols to scout for and respond to Viking attacks.

A Norse war galley of the eighth century. These ships were fast and had a shallow draft that enabled them to easily maneuver at sea as well as close to the shore or on rivers.

peror Charlemagne organized a coast guard to protect Frisia. It was only partially effective. The ships of the Franks and Saxons who lived in these parts could not protect an entire continent, and they were not fast enough to catch the Nordmanni, as the Franks called the raiders, once the enemy ships were sighted. In 834 a Viking fleet sailed up the Schelde River to the trading center of Dorestad, a busy town that had welcomed many peaceful Scandinavian merchants. From this base, the Viking king Harold led his people west and east along the low-lying coasts, eventually settling permanently in Frisia and at the mouth of the Schelde.

New Ships and New Lands

To the Irish and the Franks, the Viking raids were a catastrophe, much like a deadly storm or a volcanic explosion. The victims of these raids searched the natural world and the Bible for answers to their plight. They may not have realized that changes in Viking technology—

particularly improvements in their ships—had played the most important role in bringing the Northmen to their shores.

The ships of Scandinavia had once been narrow vessels suited only to navigating the fjords, narrow rivers, and coastal inlets of the region. (These inlets, called *vik* in the northern Germanic languages, gave the Vikings their name. To go *"a-vik-ing"* was to emerge from such an inlet to attack an enemy or to raid a foreign shore.) Around A.D. 700, Viking boatwrights began adding long, heavy keels to the bottoms of their ships. The keel gave the ships much greater stability in the rough open waters of the North Sea and the North Atlantic Ocean. Furthermore, the addition of a large mainsail made of wool cloth allowed the Vikings to drive their ships by the prevailing seasonal winds. One Icelandic saga, written centuries later, explains that "in the summer they went on Viking voyages, conquered land and divided the spoils among themselves. In the winter they stayed at home with their fathers. In those days it was easy to gain riches and honor." [8]

Viking law and custom also played a part. Violent feuds among clans, chieftains, and family members drove many Viking adventurers abroad. Likewise, food and good land were scarce and the growing season short in Scandinavia, especially in mountainous Norway. Among the Vikings, land and property passed by custom to the eldest son of each family, forcing younger brothers to acquire whatever goods or land they could by trade or by warfare. As the population of Scandinavia increased, the pressure on the existing land grew until the isolated raids of the late eighth century turned into a steady wave of migration to and colonization of the British Isles, parts of western Europe, and Russia.

Conquests in France

Neustria, the wealthy kingdom of the western Franks, attracted one of the longest and most successful of all the Viking migrations in the early 800s. The rivers of modern-day France—the Loire, the Garonne, the Rhone, the Seine, and others—provided the Vikings with an easy highway into the heart of the Frankish realm.

After the Franks' stoutest defender, Charlemagne, died in 814, no Frankish town within reach of the Viking ships was safe. The monk Ermentarius wrote at the time,

> The endless stream of Vikings never ceases to increase. Everywhere the Christians are victims of massacres, burnings, plunderings: the Vikings conquer all in their path, and no one resists them: they seize Bordeaux, Perigueux, Limoges, Angouleme and Toulouse. Angers, Tours, and Orleans are annihilated and an innumerable fleet sails up the Seine and the evil grows in the whole region. Rouen is

laid waste, plundered and burnt; Paris, Beauvais and Meaux taken, Melun's strong fortress levelled to the ground, Chartres occupied, Evreux and Bayeux plundered, and every town besieged.[9]

But the Vikings did not always meet resistance or see their intended victims flee. Many kings and lords found the fighting abilities of the Vikings useful. At the mouth of the Loire River, where the Northmen built a settlement on the island of Noirmoutier, a Frankish count named Lambert invited the Vikings to join his campaign against the nearby city of Nantes. The Vikings obliged the count by massacring the city's inhabitants on June 24, 842, while the people of Nantes were gathered to feast the birthday of St. John the Baptist.

Three years after the massacre at Nantes, a fleet of 120 Danish ships sailed past the estuary of the Seine River. Under their leader, Ragnar, the Danes rowed up the winding river as far as the city of Paris, where they met the forces of Charles the Bald, the grandson of Charlemagne. On Easter Sunday, after seeing the Vikings hang more than 100 Frankish prisoners as a sacrifice to the god Odin, Charles lost heart and gave up the fight. To save his lands from further destruction and pillage, Charles surrendered 7,000 pounds of silver to the Danes.

This huge ransom set a precedent for the other lords and rulers of Europe, who now made it a custom to simply bribe the Vikings to leave their lands in peace. The offers of *Danegeld* over the next 150 years amounted to many thousands of pounds of silver coins as well as gold, jewelry, and precious stones. The ransoms were carried off to workshops in Scandinavia and to Viking colonies in the British Isles and western Europe, where the silver was melted down and crafted into jewelry and ornaments by Viking metalsmiths.

The Land of the Northmen

One of the largest such Viking ransoms was paid to the Danish chief Hrolf, also known as Rollo. This leader and his men proved such a menace to northwestern Europe that King Charles the Simple, the grandson of Charles the Bald, offered an entire province around the mouth of the Seine River in exchange for peace and a military alliance. This agreement, set forth in the Treaty of St. Clair-sur-Epte in 911, led to the founding of the Viking kingdom of Normandy ("land of the Northmen").

Over the next few generations, Rollo's Danes adopted the language and customs of the western Franks, the ancestors of the modern French nation. Intermarriage between Vikings and Franks brought about a distinct Norman society, whose leaders built one of the most powerful states in medieval Europe. Norman adventurers set out to conquer distant parts of Europe and the Mediterranean

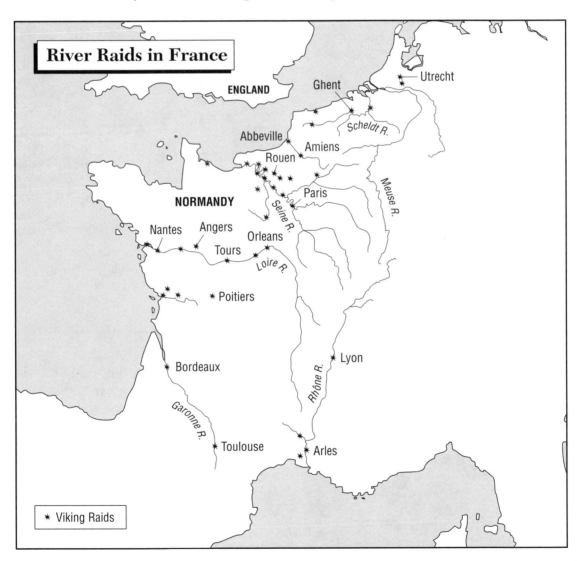

River Raids in France

ENGLAND
Ghent
Utrecht
Abbeville
Amiens
Scheldt R.
Rouen
NORMANDY
Seine R.
Paris
Meuse R.
Nantes
Angers
Orleans
Tours
Loire R.
Poitiers
Bordeaux
Garonne R.
Lyon
Rhône R.
Toulouse
Arles

* Viking Raids

region, bringing with them word of their newly adopted faith, Christianity. As historian Peter Brent writes,

> Northmen became ferocious missionaries, but although they preached with sword-edge rather than Bible, with mundane threat rather than heavenly promise, they made their converts. [They] ordered baptism as other rulers did military service or some outrageous tax; after their time, however, Christianity was the established religion of their peoples. The very restlessness of Scandinavian voyagers, their endless flitting to and fro before the various winds of their years, helped to carry this new message about the world.[10]

Rollo and his fleet attack Paris. Eager to avoid continual conflict, Frankish leaders organized a treaty with Rollo that granted him a kingdom in France. That kingdom was dubbed Normandy after the Norsemen who settled there.

Relations with the Franks eventually led the Normans to accept Christianity. Here, King Rollo is baptized into the new faith.

The Danelaw

Danish Vikings also found a permanent home on the mainland of Great Britain. In Scandinavia they had used ships to navigate the many small islands of the Danish seas; in England they used a network of roads built during Roman times to move swiftly through the northern and eastern regions to overwhelm the Anglo-Saxon kingdoms. In 869 the king of East Anglia, Edmund, was tortured and murdered by Vikings under the command of Guthrum. Another group of Vikings established their own kingdom in Northumbria in 876.

In 878, however, King Alfred of Wessex, in southern England, defeated the Danes at the Battle of Aethandune. To protect his realm, Alfred had built fortifications in many towns of Wessex as well as a strong defensive fleet. Many Viking raids were stopped at the coast; their leaders were killed and the ships' crews were driven back to the sea. But Alfred also realized that he could not expel the Vikings permanently from Britain. In 886 he struck a deal with Guthrum. Wessex would remain independent; the regions of northern and eastern England already under Viking control would be given up to the Danes. Guthrum, in turn, denounced the Norse gods and was baptized into the Christian faith. The territory under Viking control in Britain became known as the Danelaw.

The Rus

An eastern wave of Viking migration began around the coasts of the Baltic Sea in the middle of the ninth century. After building towns and depots along the Baltic's southern shore, Swedish traders—known as the "Rus"—moved on to the waterways that carried them to the Volga and the Dnieper Rivers, the ancient highways of this part of Europe. A great trading center was raised at Staraya Ladoga, south of Lake Ladoga. From there the Rus rowed and portaged their vessels south to the Black Sea, the Caspian Sea, and the city of Constantinople, capital of the Byzantine Empire and the richest city in Europe.

The Slavs who lived in the forests and plains of this region often found themselves involved in violent civil quarrels. The Swedish Vikings who now appeared offered a chance to settle their conflicts. In the late ninth century, according to legend, the Slavs invited Rurik, leader of the Rus, to rule over them.

Rurik accepted the invitation and established a capital at Novgorod. In a few years, Rurik had extended his domain south, while his fellow Rus warriors, Askold and Dir, built the city of Kiev on the Dnieper River. In 882 Prince Oleg of Novgorod, a descendant of Rurik, attacked and conquered Kiev. Oleg killed Askold and Dir and founded the principality of Russia.

With the founding of a united, more peaceful realm, the great rivers and portages of Russia grew even busier. Scandinavian traders brought "their beaverskins and black fox and swords from the furthest parts of their land down to the Black Sea," wrote the Arab historian Ibn Khurdadhbih. "The Greek Emperor charges tithe on their goods. They

Swedish chieftain Rurik lands on the Baltic coast. At the request of quarreling Slavs, Rurik came to eastern Europe to pacify and rule over the people of the region.

reach the Caspian and take ship again. Sometimes they bring their wares by camel from Jurjan to Baghdad, where Slavonic eunuchs interpret for them. They say they are Christian."[11] The traders brought back plunder, trade goods, and more than eighty thousand Arab coins dating to the ninth and tenth centuries. The flood of goods from the south made the Swedish island of Gotland, in the Baltic Sea, a wealthy trading center. Today, hordes of coins and jewelry from Russia and the Middle East have been unearthed on Gotland.

On to Miklagard

The Rus, like other Vikings, still gave their highest praise and honors not to wealth but to fighting skill. Unlike some other Viking settlers in Europe, however, the Rus did not leave behind their warlike heritage after settling their new land. Four times during the late ninth and early tenth century, the Rus staged surprise raids on Constantinople, which the Rus called Miklagard ("great city").

To the people of Constantinople, the worst aspect of the Vikings was not their violence or their greed but rather their paganism. Non-Christians were considered immoral, uncontrollable, almost subhuman beings without any redeeming virtues such as reason, humility, or mercy. In one of his sermons, Photius, the patriarch of the Eastern Christian church of Byzantium, told his followers that "an obscure nation . . . dwelling somewhere far from our country, barbarous, nomadic, armed with arrogance has suddenly, in the twinkling of an eye, like a wave of the sea, poured over our frontiers, and as a wild boar has devoured the inhabitants of the land like grass."[12]

To the Byzantine emperors, the Rus appeared terrifying yet useful. By treaty in 911, the Rus were allowed to serve as soldiers in the Byzantine army. Later in the century, the emperor enlisted a group of Rus warriors to

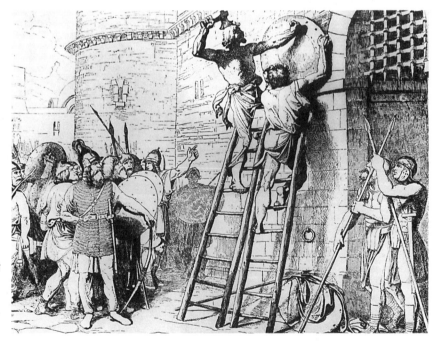

Prince Oleg nails his shield to the wall of Constantinople. After unsuccessful raids against the Byzantine capital, the Rus eked out an alliance with the defenders, and eventually several Vikings served in the city's elite guard.

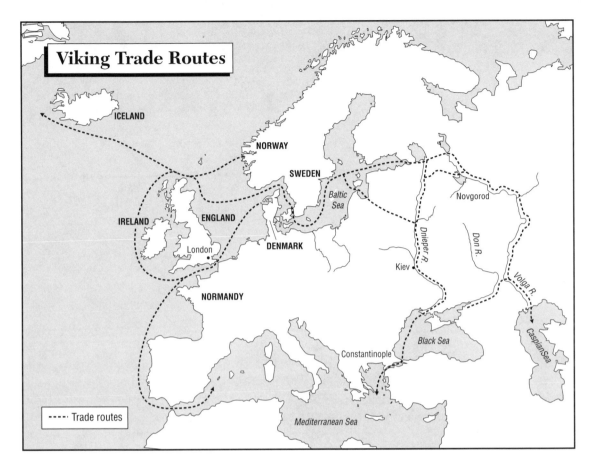

Viking Trade Routes

ICELAND

NORWAY

SWEDEN

Baltic
Sea

Novgorod

IRELAND

ENGLAND

London

DENMARK

Dnieper R.

Don R.

Kiev

Volga R.

NORMANDY

Caspian Sea

Black Sea

Constantinople

Mediterranean Sea

- - - - Trade routes

help put down an uprising. These Rus proved to be such admirable fighters that the emperor organized them into an elite mercenary corps known as the Varangian Guard. They were awarded the right to free meat, fish, bread, and wine, as well as free baths. The Varangians also earned sails, ropes, wood, and other supplies for their ships, which they employed for further bloody conquest and raiding in the eastern Mediterranean.

The Norman Conquest and the End of the Viking Age

In Great Britain, meanwhile, the Anglo-Saxon nobles and the rulers of the Danelaw found they could not live in peace, despite Alfred's treaty with Guthrum. Another invasion arrived from Denmark in 994 under Sweyn I Forkbeard; in 1016 Sweyn's son Canute defeated King Aethelred of Wessex. Sixty years later, when the English king Edward the Confessor died, the struggle for power in England brought the Normans to Britain under their leader William the Conqueror, the great-great-great-great-grandson of the Danish king Rollo. In 1066 William defeated his rivals at the Battle of Hastings and founded the Norman dynasty, the beginnings of the modern English kingdom.

To modern historians, the Battle of Hastings marks the end of the Viking age. Viking raids on Europe became a thing of the past,

The Vikings and Europe

Historians Else Roesdahl and David M. Wilson, in their book *From Viking to Crusader: The Scandinavians and Europe, 800–1200*, note that the Vikings contributed much to the history and culture of medieval Europe.

"The Scandinavians not only took, they also gave. The Viking raids brought enormous wealth to the North along with new impulses which were to provide the background for radical changes in Nordic society in the following period. Their influences on Europe include their language, personal names, and place-names, all of which modified those of England, Ireland and Normandy. Normandy acquired a Scandinavian ruling dynasty and a political system from which base it became one of the greatest powers in eleventh and twelfth-century Europe. The rulers of the Russian kingdom with its capital in Kiev—to become the centre of the Russian state—were also of Nordic origin. . . . Many places where Scandinavians settled are still distinctive through their structures of ownership, land-use, or political systems."

while unified kingdoms were set up in Denmark, Sweden, and Norway. The Scandinavians gradually assimilated into the native societies of England, Normandy, Russia, and other lands where they had settled. Christianization—sometimes peaceful, sometimes violent—brought down the pagan gods among the people of Scandinavia, while the Scandinavians themselves joined crusades to liberate the holy land from the Muslims. Prince Vladimir of Kiev forcefully converted the Russians to Christianity in 988; Sweden, the last Scandinavian nation to accept Christianity, converted by the eleventh century.

Eventually, the deeds and misdeeds of the Vikings passed into distant memory for the people of Europe. In Scandinavia these same events became the inspiration for legends and sagas that made up the heart of national myths, much as the deeds of the pilgrims and the early European colonists make up an important historical myth for the people of the United States. Historians who study the Middle Ages see the Vikings as a minor subject and usually pass them by with a brief mention of the raids and the death and destruction they caused. H. G. Wells, in his book *The Outline of History*, captures this attitude by declaring simply, "Their animus against the Cross and against monks and nuns was extreme. They delighted in the burning of monasteries and nunneries and the slaughter of their inmates."[13]

Yet in many ways, everyday life among the Vikings remains a mystery. No written works of this age have survived to describe the Vikings in their own words—only a handful of poems and thousands of short runic inscriptions that give few details. The Norse sagas of a later age, the chronicles of Europeans who saw the Vikings as their enemies, and the evidence of archaeology must now tell the tale. Nevertheless, the evidence that does exist recounts many fascinating and surprising details about a people who played an important role in the history of Europe.

Viking Ships, Raiding, and Warfare

The Vikings might have remained a little-known pagan society, living on the distant, northern edge of Europe, if it had not been for their great skill as boatwrights and as oceanic sailors. By the ninth century, when the Vikings were harrying the rest of Europe and the Mediterranean basin, the northerners were sailing the world's fastest and most durable ships and voyaging farther than any other sailors in Europe. Without these sturdy "longships," Viking raiding and colonization would have been impossible. More than any single person, place, or event, these ships represent and define the Vikings.

Changes at Sea

Ever since the first migrations into Scandinavia, the people living there had used wooden boats to travel. Because there were few roads or trails over the mountains of Norway, and there were so many lakes and other waterways in Sweden, it was often necessary or easiest to sail to a given destination (the islands of Denmark made water travel necessary as well). The rivers, lakes, and fjords of the region, and the rough climate, demanded great skill in navigation and seamanship. But ships sailing under oar power alone could travel no

A stone carving showing a Viking longship. The longship became a symbol of the Vikings because these vessels were the primary means by which Norse culture was brought in contact with the rest of Europe.

more than a day or two in open seas, where steep waves would quickly exhaust rowers and swamp their boats.

Sometime in the eighth century, the Vikings made important changes in the way they designed their ships. A keel was added to steady the ships in heavy seas. A large rectangular sail was added to boats that were formerly powered by rowing, allowing crews to stow their oars and sail swiftly before the wind across large stretches of open sea. Made of wool, the sail hung from a tall mast that was set into a heavy block that rested in the center of the ship. Decorated with a unique pattern of squares, stripes, or diamonds, the sail served as a personal signboard that announced the presence of a Viking king or chieftain to his friends and foes.

Building a Viking Ship

To build a Viking longship, a boatwright had to begin with the longest and heaviest part: its oaken keel. The keel had to be straight, without imperfections, and made from a single piece of wood. Making the keel deeper under the center of the ship helped the boat to resist the tug of underwater currents. Making it shallow under the bow and stern helped the crew to more easily turn and maneuver the vessel.

For the sides of the ships, the Vikings used thick vertical ribs and horizontal strakes, or long, sturdy oaken planks. The strakes were set in rows, with each row slightly overlapping the row beneath it. They were shaped with an iron-edged adze and then either lashed with thick roots to the ribs of the boat or fastened to the ribs with iron rivets. The lashes kept the boat watertight while allowing the strakes to move and bend slightly when hit by heavy seas (rivets, when used, made the ship much more rigid).

At the rear of the boat, always on the right side, a side rudder was used for steering. (The Norse word *styra,* meaning "to steer," survives in modern English as *starboard,* which means the right-hand side of a boat, when viewed from the back.) The steersman moved the rudder with a wooden tiller. The rudder could be raised quickly in shallow water,

A Viking longship on a trading mission. The ships could be powered either by their rectangular sail or by their banks of oars.

The Oseberg longship is one of the few preserved Viking vessels. The long strakes that make up the sides are visible, as well as the high, curved stern.

allowing the boats to be run completely up on a beach. The side rudder also allowed the strakes to curve upward at the stern, where the fixed rudders on other kinds of boats were placed. This symmetrical design—curving upward at both ends—served another important purpose: The raised bow and stern prevented waves from breaking into the boat in rough weather.

At Sea and in Harbor

Inside the ships, the crew sat on sea chests or on sturdy cross beams that were fastened to the sides. The chests held their clothing, weapons, food, water, and extra rope, tools, and sailcloth. Oars were stowed along the center bottom of the hull. The longships had little room for cargo—they were fighting ships, not trading vessels (the hafskip, a much shorter but broader vessel, had been designed for that purpose).

Once the ship was rowed out of the harbor or fjord, the sail was raised on its mast. To make up for a relatively short mast, the sails were made extremely long, as wide as seventy feet. To keep the sail from billowing back and forth in a heavy wind, wooden spars were attached to the lower edges of the sails from the bulwarks (sides), pushing the sail outward and holding it steady.

To maneuver in narrow rivers or along coasts, the crew could lower the sail as well as the mast, which then rested in wooden crutches on the deck. Oars were passed through small openings near the top of the hull. Along the side of some ships stood a row of round shields. The shields were only in place for ceremony or display, as they prevented the crew from passing their oars through the hull and rowing the boat.

The shallow draft (underwater depth) of Viking ships allowed their crews to run them directly onto beaches. Using this technique, the raiders could strike suddenly and quickly escape any pursuers, if necessary. Historian James Graham-Campbell explains:

Viking shipbuilders had perfected reliable sailing ships that had no need of deep water, safe anchorages, or quaysides. Their construction and shallow draught allowed them to use any sloping beach as their harbour and to maneuver in waters unsuitable for most European

Viking Ships, Raiding, and Warfare **25**

vessels of that time. No wonder that surprise was felt, along with terror and rage, at such raids.[14]

The Dragon Ship

A Viking's ship represented his wealth, bravery, and ruthlessness in battle. The shields, painted sails, and carved monsters were intended to frighten and subdue enemies, and on the rivers and coasts of Europe, they sometimes prompted surrender even before a battle was begun. The imaginary beasts that decorated the curving prows of these ships

The dragon head, the colorful sails, and the rows of shields along the sides of the vessel made the dragon ship an awesome sight that effectively terrorized onlookers.

gave them the nickname "dragon ships" and proved to be an effective medieval form of psychological warfare.

One of the greatest of all dragon ships belonged to Harold Hardraade, or Harold the Ruthless, of eleventh-century Norway. The ship was described by the Icelandic poet Snorri Sturluson in *King Harald's Saga:*

> It was much broader than normal warships . . . and most carefully built in every detail. Its prow had a dragon's head, and the stern had a dragon's tail, and the bows were inlaid with gold. It had thirty-five pairs of rowing benches, with plenty of space between each; it was indeed a magnificent vessel.[15]

Viking Raiding

The Vikings used their longships to raid nearly every corner of Europe, from Ireland to France, Spain, Italy, the Baltic Coast, and along the rivers of central Europe. Historians continue to debate the theories that explain this sudden outburst of warfare and piracy. Some historians believe a shortage of land in Scandinavia, or civil wars, drove certain groups out of their homeland. Noting that the number of graves sharply increases at the beginning of the Viking period, others contend that the region experienced a population explosion, which may have prompted Danes, Norwegians, and Swedes to set out across the sea in search of treasure as well as new land to cultivate and settle.

Whatever the reasons for Viking raids, they had occurred for centuries in Scandinavia, where chiefs attacked rivals living across mountain ranges or along distant yet familiar coasts. Nor was hit-and-run warfare new to Europe at the time. As historian P. H. Sawyer notes, "The Viking raids were not so

An animal head carving for the prow of a Viking longship. Such fearsome visages were designed to intimidate enemies.

very different from the raids of Saxons on the Franks or the Frankish attacks on the Saxons and the Avars. Charlemagne was certainly filled with a sense of Christian mission, but he too was compelled by the need to reward his followers with land and treasure." There was one important difference: "When the Vikings came, there was little chance of any warning, and this meant that there was little time to assemble opposition. Equally, their way of retreat was often safe, certainly from pursuit." [16]

The Raiding Season

The raids on foreign lands were often organized by a Viking chieftain, who invited the able-bodied warriors of his district to join expeditions during the fair sailing season. One Icelandic saga recounts the seasonal planning of Svein Asleifarson, who owned a large farm in the Orkney Islands:

The Accidental Discovery of America

The Vikings were the best navigators of Europe, but they also suffered the dangers of sailing in the rough, stormy northern seas. Many Vikings died at sea; entire expeditions of colonists or raiders were lost without a trace. The thick fogs and unpredictable winds of the North Atlantic forced ships off course, sometimes for great distances, to land on unfamiliar territory. In his book *The Viking World*, writer James Graham-Campbell describes the troubles of one Viking sailor who brought about the first European "discovery" of America.

"As accident and chance had led to the discovery of Greenland, so the story continues. When Bjarni Herjolfsson sighted a western land that was flat and covered with woods, it was clear that this was not the Greenland for which he had set sail from Iceland. He was attempting to follow his parents, who had sailed that year with Erik the Red to settle there, when he got lost in foggy seas, blown off course by north winds. Thus, in about 985, Bjarni was probably the first Norseman to sight America—maybe indeed the first European to do so, unless one believes that St. Brendan or some other Irish monk achieved this in a leather boat (and returned to tell the tale). But Bjarni never stepped ashore for he was no explorer, rather a man with a cargo to deliver in Greenland, where he eventually landed."

In the spring he had more than enough to occupy him, with a great deal of seed to sow. . . . Then, when that job was done, he would go off plundering in the Hebrides and in Ireland on what he called his "spring trip," then back home just after midsummer, where he stayed till the cornfields had been reaped and the grain was safely in. After that he would go off raiding again till the first month of winter was ended. This he used to call his "autumn trip."[17]

The most powerful of these chieftains, such as the Vestfaldingi kings of the Oslo fjord in Norway, could raise thousands of well-armed warriors on seasonal raiding parties. These parties were usually successful, as the raiders had the crucial element of surprise. In fleets of up to several dozen ships, they struck without giving defenders enough time to summon help or to put in place adequate defenses. They attacked monasteries and coastal villages that were weakly defended, killing without mercy and taking only those prisoners whom they intended to hold for ransom or sell as slaves. The main object of these raids, however, was not murder; it was treasure in the form of gold and silver jewelry and coins and religious objects such as crosses, reliquaries, and chalices.

Raiding Turns to Migration

The first Viking raids on Britain and Europe took place in the late spring. Norwegians sailed directly across the North Sea to the northern coasts of Britain, the Shetland Islands, and Ireland. The Danes sailed west to southern England and to the northern and western coasts of France. In the fall the raiders returned home to their farms and villages to tend their livestock and crops and spread tall tales about their bravery in foreign lands.

Viking fleets of the most powerful chieftains were often large. Thousands of warriors would make the voyages to plunder distant lands and then return victorious to their Scandinavian homes.

Their improved ships allowed the Vikings to make the long-distance raids and trading voyages that brought them as far as the Middle East and across the Atlantic Ocean. To undertake these journeys, however, the Vikings had to match the skills of their boatwrights with excellent seamanship. They had no compasses, sextants, or other navigational instruments of any kind. They had no charts of tides, water depth, or the position of the sun, moon, and stars at certain times of the day and night. They sailed without maps, using instead the familiar patterns of currents and the winds that they had learned and passed down to the next generation of navigators.

In the *Dictionary of the Middle Ages*, author Bruce Gelsinger describes the Viking practice of latitude sailing.

"Whenever new land in the west was discovered—progressively, the Faeroes, Iceland, and Greenland—the height there of the sun at midday would be ascertained several times during the sailing season; when traveling from Norway, which faces all of these places, a sailor would first sail up or down the Atlantic coast to the point where the sun's altitude was the same, then make his departure across the sea. Latitude sailing was also indirectly useful for north-south sailings. For instance, if an Icelander knew the height of the midday sun in northern Ireland at various times during the sailing season, he could sail south of his island until he reached the latitude of Ireland, then sail east until he struck land."

To get their bearings near land, the Vikings used familiar clues such as patterns of clouds or the direction and temperature of certain sea currents. Flights of certain birds and schools of whales might show that land was near. Surprisingly far out at sea, land could be smelled, and fresh water from a large outflowing river could be tasted in the seawater. Some Viking ships carried domesticated ravens that could be sent out in search of land. When land was finally sighted, and the crew intended to build a settlement, posts would be thrown overboard and allowed to float to shore. The settlers would build their colony wherever they landed.

Around 840, however, the Vikings began setting up permanent island settlements along the coasts of foreign territories: Lambay Island at the mouth of the Liffey River in Ireland, the island of Noirmoutier at the mouth of the Loire on the Atlantic coast of France, and Walcheren in the Schelde River in Frisia. Groups of raiders retired for the winter at these settlements and planned for the next year's activities, since it was easier to raid from such enclaves than to sail across the open seas from Norway or Denmark.

Viking attacks reached their peak in the mid to late ninth century, when the Scandinavians brought down entire kingdoms in Britain and on the European continent with their piracy and pillaging. As historian Robert Wernick writes,

Under the weight of the Viking assault, the petty kingdoms of Northumbria, East Anglia, and Mercia collapsed one by one, their strength drained, their royal lineage extinguished. By 880 only one Anglo-Saxon kingdom survived, Wessex in the southwest.[18]

The annual raids had turned into large-scale, national migrations. A new generation of Vikings was migrating in search of land on which to build farms and settle permanently. Norwegians settled in the Shetland and Faeroe Islands; Danes settled in Northumbria in eastern Great Britain; and both Danes and Norwegians settled in Ireland.

Fighting in the Viking Age

Like soldiers in the rest of Europe during the Middle Ages, the Vikings fought in close, intimate battles. Tactics were simple; there was little strategic maneuvering. Each side tried to fight from the high ground and to avoid obstacles such as rivers, cliffs, and the sea. While still far apart, the two sides positioned their archers, if they were present, in front to fire a great volley of arrows. As the armies moved closer, they began hurling spears and finally engaged in hand-to-hand combat. Axes, swords, knives, and spears clashed against wooden shields, iron helmets, and suits of heavy chain mail.

Viking kings and chieftains led their soldiers from the front lines. Their victory over the opponent's leader, or their death, decided the battle, as did the capture or loss of a symbolic royal banner. During one eleventh-century battle, as a saga poet describes it,

> King Harald . . . led a charge into the thickest of the fighting. [He] rushed forward ahead of his troops, fighting two-handed. Neither helmets nor coats of mail could withstand him, and everyone in his path gave way before him. . . . But now Harald Sigurdsson was struck in the throat by an arrow, and this was his death wound. He fell, and with him fell all

The Berserker

The most fearsome Viking warrior was the berserker. Berserkers made up a unique and specially trained fighting class of their own, much like the samurai of Imperial Japan or the modern U.S. Navy SEALS. The berserker derived his skill from a dedication to the god Odin, the patron of all warriors, and, according to some historians, from the use of hallucinogenic plants.

The word berserk comes from the Norse word for "bear-shirt," which according to legend, was the garment worn by berserkers in battle (others claim they simply fought naked). Historian Robert Wernick describes these warriors in his book *The Vikings*.

"[The berserkers] would roll their eyes, bite the edge of their shields and utter animal howls. They would rush toward their adversaries without thought of pain or danger, sometimes without any protective armor. . . . Not every Viking fought that way, of course. Modern scholars suggest that such fantastic behavior may have been the result of drunken rages brought on by great drafts of ale or wine just before combat, of paranoia or possibly of genetic flaws in individuals.

Whatever the cause, a number of Vikings—no one knows the percentage—did go berserk when they fought. And some kings and jarls found it useful to have bodyguards made up of these men, or to use them as shock troops or simply to spread terror wherever they went."

those who had advanced with him, except for those who retreated with the royal standard.[19]

The Vikings customarily raided and fought in small companies; they did best in smaller battles in which skill in hand-to-hand fighting was the key to victory. But some Viking leaders could assemble large, well-provisioned forces that could withstand long sieges. In 885, under Siegfried and Orm, seven hundred Viking ships and their crews attacked the metropolis of Paris, which lay behind thick stone walls on an island in the Seine River. Historian Robert Wernick describes the scene:

> In moments the air was a blizzard of arrows. The stones of the fortress towers resounded with the clang of thousands of spears hurled against them, and after the Vikings flung flaming torches at the battlements the whole city was ablaze. For all the ferocity of the attack, the Vikings did not succeed in taking Paris. But they did invest both banks of the river, and from there they held the city under siege for the better part of a year, simultaneously ravaging the French countryside for miles around.[20]

Those who faced a Viking attack or raid could expect no mercy. Ordinarily, when an enemy was defeated, no prisoners were taken (a few might be captured and sold or kept as slaves). Those who could not escape, were wounded, fell disarmed to the ground, or were exhausted could expect only a quick death by decapitation. If the attack was directed against a settlement, it was customary to loot and then burn farms, homes, workshops—any structures left standing. Anyone unlucky enough to be trapped inside would be burned as well.

Norsemen besieging Paris in 885. Although hit-and-run raids were common for Vikings, some Norse chieftains were able to raise large forces that could lay siege to cities or combat the standing armies of European rulers.

Horik and the Jomsvikings

Gradually the Vikings assembled themselves into larger and more disciplined fighting forces. The Danish king Horik, who ruled from 827 to 854, sought to organize this helter-skelter piracy into "national" raids that could subdue large, well-defended cities. (This was also a way for Horik to unite the feuding clans and chieftains of his realm.) In 845 the Danes collected large fleets of warships to sail up the Elbe and the Seine to attack Hamburg and Paris. In 878 the most powerful Viking army of all time gathered at the mouth of the Schelde River. This horde spent thirteen years burning and looting throughout northern France and western Germany before being stopped by a plague in 892.

Viking warriors also established independent fighting clans that used their small territories as bases for raiding and collecting tribute. One such group was the Jomsvikings,

A segment of the Bayeux tapestry shows a Viking ship off the English coast. As the Viking raiders established settlements in conquered regions, their armies grew in size. This ship was part of the larger army that eventually challenged the standing army of King Harold II of England.

Women Warriors

With stirring description and nonstop action, the twelfth- and thirteenth-century sagas of Iceland, written after the end of the Viking age, recount the heroic deeds of explorers, warriors, and kings of bygone Scandinavia. In a few instances, these sagas also tell of the exploits of strong and brave women. Prudence Jones and Nigel Pennick, in their book *A History of Pagan Europe*, quote one of these tales, the *Sogubrot*, as follows:

"The Shield Maiden Vebjorg made fierce attacks on the Swedes and Goths; she attacked the champion Soknarskoti; she had trained herself as well to use the helmet, mail-shirt, and sword, [and] she was one of the foremost in knighthood. She dealt the champion heavy blows and attacked him for a long time, and with a heavy blow at his cheek cut through his jaw and chin; he put his beard in his mouth and bit it, thus holding up his chin. She performed many great feats of arms. Later, Thorkel the Stubborn, a champion of Hring, met her and they attacked each other fiercely. Finally, with great courage, she fell, covered with wounds."

who lived on the coast of the Baltic Sea. The Jomsvikings kept strict discipline among themselves, admitted no member younger than eighteen or older than fifty, and held all their goods in common. They emerged from their outpost each summer to attack their enemies and plunder the nearby countryside.

Late in the Viking era, powerful kings raised armies of warriors, ships, and cavalry from among the nobles and peasants they ruled. These were the first national "armies" of Scandinavia, used for large-scale foreign conquest. One of the last great Viking campaigns was led by Harold Hardraade, a Norwegian who fought in the Varangian Guard and spent many years at the head of a fearsome raiding army in the Mediterranean. In 1066 Harold gathered Norwegians, Orkney islanders, and allies led by the English noble Tostig, the rival brother of King Harold II. Harold Hardraade brought this army south along the coast of England, marched inland, and conquered the city of York. East of the city, however, he was met by King Harold, who defeated the Norwegian at the Battle of Stamford Bridge. After King Harold was defeated by William the Conqueror at the Battle of Hastings on October 14, 1066, William began the Norman Conquest of England, an event that also marked the end of the Viking age.

Viking Society

Behind the tall tales and legends of the Vikings lay the more complex reality of Viking society. The Vikings divided themselves into several distinct social classes and organized themselves according to many different, long-held customs of self-government and justice. Although most of the Viking names that have survived ten or more centuries belong to kings or great chieftains, the Vikings themselves saw their clans and families as the most important segment of their society—the only one, in the end, to which they owed their service and their loyalty.

Viking Families

The Vikings held no allegiance to a central government or to a national king who ruled by right of inheritance over a far-flung realm. They had no flags or national borders. Instead, they saw themselves as part of a clan that provided security and a family that provided sustenance and shelter. According to tradition, the head of the farmstead, or *bondi,* was a local patriarch who made the most important decisions and who was honored by holding a place in the highest seat in the central hall. Their extended families might also include brothers, sisters, cousins, and grandparents who lived on a single farm or a group of farmsteads that made up a village.

The family and their kin living nearby saw themselves as almost a sovereign unit, apart from most outside control and influence. There were no police, jails, written laws or law courts; the family had to protect its land and possessions as best it could. The members of the family gathered riches when possible, carried out legal judgments passed in their favor by the local assembly, and helped protect the clan in times of strife. It was also the family's responsibility to conduct funerals and to carve memorials to the dead. Johannes Brondsted explains:

> The family unit was indispensable in death as well as life; as after all it was the family which built and preserved the grave, mound, or cemetery, however the dead were disposed of. Here the family kept its dead, and here in a sense they lived on, even if they visited Valhalla or Heaven in between. Or the dead might live on within a holy mountain or hill near the ancestral farm. The dead were always with the family, and for that reason it was a family obligation always to maintain the grave or the burial mound in good order so that the departed would never feel so forsaken as to be obliged to become a vengeful ghost. A walker-after-death was terrible and dangerous, and the only course open to the relatives would be to break open his grave and kill him a second time.[21]

Marriage Among the Vikings

One of the best opportunities for Viking households to increase their wealth and power was through the marriage of sons and daughters. For this reason, marriages were often arranged between two families. The marriage agreement included the terms of the bride's bride-price (a payment made to the bride's family), or, later in the Viking age, the dowry (goods donated by the bride's family to the marriage). Powerful landowners and chieftains used marriages to forge alliances with others of their class. And in some places, polygamy was practiced by men wealthy enough to support more than one wife. Ecclesiastical historian Adam of Bremen, writing during the eleventh century, records that among the Swedes, "every man, each according to his means, has two, three or more wives at a time; the wealthy and the nobles have numerous wives. The sons of all these unions are accepted as legitimate."[22]

Nevertheless, during the Viking era women had as much independence and authority in Scandinavia as anywhere else in Europe. Although the affairs of the local assembly, foreign warfare, and trading were considered men's concerns, women held much authority in managing the farm and the household. When husbands traveled abroad, wives were often left to manage farms and households entirely on their own. Women also carved runes (and raised runestones) to memorialize themselves or the dead. In addition, women could own property; and, when settling a new land, they had the right to claim land of their own. Viking wives also had the right to divorce their husbands. In the case of divorce, according to some historians, the dowry brought to the household by the bride was returned to her.

Thralls and *Karls*

One popular image of the Vikings describes them as a democratic, egalitarian society of hardy farmers, artisans, and sailors. But the Vikings did not necessarily enjoy equal opportunity; instead, they lived on the rungs of a rigid social ladder, at the bottom of which

A Viking gravesite. Such memorials were well tended by relatives because the Norse feared that their departed would return as ghosts if they were not properly remembered and honored.

The karls or landless commoners were eager to undertake raiding missions because the profits of such ventures helped them afford property and thus rise in social status.

stood the thralls. These were slaves who owned no property and had no legal rights whatsoever. Many of them were captives from foreign raiding or prisoners of civil wars within Scandinavia; others were servants who sold themselves into a household for a certain length of time, perhaps to pay off a debt. They carried out the most wearying and most difficult tasks: ploughing of unbroken sod, digging wells or ditches, herding livestock, cutting or hauling logs from the forests. They could be sold at any time, but in some places they also could work themselves out of thralldom with enough years of service and raise themselves to the status of *karls.*

The Viking *karls* were free peasants: farmers, artisans, traders, or soldiers, who might work for a wealthy family or a company of raiders, or in a city as an apprentice to an iron-

smith or a boatwright. A *karl,* as well as a jarl, or chieftain, had the right to debate and vote at the *thing,* or assembly, where the laws were argued, issues decided, and legal judgments given. But the greatest ambition of the Viking *karl* was to acquire property, as fertile land was rare and considered the only true measure of a Viking's wealth. Eventually, with the help of successful trading or raids abroad and mastery over his neighbors, the landowning *karl* might become a jarl.

Jarls and Kings

Jarls were the wealthiest and most powerful landowners in any region, whether it be a certain stretch of coast, an isolated mountain valley, or a group of farming settlements. If strong enough, the jarl could exact tribute from the landowners in his region as well as those living nearby. One Norwegian chieftain, Othere, exacted tribute from the Lapps, nomadic hunters and fishermen who lived in the far north of his lands. According to one ninth-century English report, the Lapps paid in the form of

> skins of beasts, the feathers of birds, whale-bone, and ship-ropes made from walrus-hide and sealskin. Each pays according to his rank. The highest in ranks has to pay fifteen marten skins, five reindeer skins, one bear skin, and ten measures of feathers, and a jacket of bearskin or otterskin and two ship ropes. Each of these must be sixty ells long, one made from walrus-hide, the other from seal.[23]

Jarls who were able to raise a bodyguard and a permanent fleet of ships, to hold large tracts of land through loyalty and service of other landowners, to carry out successful raids, and to control trade on the roads and sea lanes through their region raised themselves to the status of king. But the kings of the Vikings had to rule by force of personality and by their ability as warriors. There were no elections among the Vikings, and the succession of a son to the kingship of his father could easily be challenged. The *karls* who worked the land offered only their loyalty in wartime and their aid on foreign expeditions; they considered taxes and tribute to a king a form of vassalage, fit only for thralls and conquered people, not for a free Viking.

Some of the Viking kings, such as those who ruled the Vestfold area of Norway, were rich enough to own several large halls and estates, which they visited at different times of the year. They gathered large groups of loyal soldiers who were outfitted with the best arms,

Origins of the Viking Thralls

The Vikings created many different tales and myths to explain the condition of the world and of their own society. In his book *The Norsemen,* author Eric Oxenstierna recites "The Lay of Rig," an old Norse poem that describes how the class of thralls came about.

> A swarthy boy was born to Edda
> She sprinkled water on him called him Tral (Slave)
> Black were his nails his face was ugly
> Gnarled were his joints crooked his back
> Thick were his fingers and his feet were long. . . .

Tral meets a girl, but there is no mention of marriage.

> They chattered and whispered the livelong day
> Boy and wench and lay together
> Content in their hut they had a brood.
>
> The boys were called: Cattle-boy, Blusterer
> Lout, Hunchback, Concubine-Keeper, Sluggard
> Clod, Knocknees, Squarehead, Brat
> Horse-fly, Paunchy They laid fences,
> Herded the goats, dug for peat. . . .
>
> The daughters were called: Clumsy girl, Fat-One,
> Spindly-legs, Kitchen-maid,
> Slattern and Fat-legs,
> Servant-girl, Hasty, and Beanpole.
> From them are sprung the class of thralls.

armor, ships, and horses, who feasted at the king's table, and who were granted estates of their own to farm or to rent as they pleased. (They also swore to fight wherever the king might lead them.) The kings were considered descendants of the pagan gods and heroes, but they were also subject to the jealous intrigues of those whom they ruled. Assassination and civil war were common events in the Viking world, as few landowners paid much respect to the idea of dynasties or royal families.

A few kings who were able to defeat all of their rivals, claim victories in foreign wars, and hold widespread loyalty among their sub-jects rose to the status of national monarchs. The first such kings were Harold I Hårfager in Norway (during the 870s), Sweyn I Fork-beard in Denmark (985), and Olaf Skautko-nung in Sweden (993). But royal dynasties did not begin in Scandinavia until after the end of the Viking age.

The *Thing:* Administrators of Law

More important than kings and jarls to the day-to-day governing and justice among the

The castle of a Norse king. The few Vikings who raised themselves to the level of kings did so through a show of strength or by the force of their personality.

Vikings was the *thing*, an assembly of free adult men. The *thing* may have begun in wartime, when the Vikings assembled their soldiers and arms at a central meeting point. Later, this place was used to debate and decide on the laws and justice, to resolve conflicts, and to make important decisions. The assembly place might be a mound, a high hill, or in the shadow of a prominent rock. Such a *thing-hill* still exists on the Isle of Man and continues to be used for public ceremonies.

The *thing* survived the Viking age and continued its administration of laws that were codified and set down in writing. Much larger regional assemblies, known as *landthings*, were convened to decide national issues such as the election of kings or a declaration of war against a neighboring country. But well into medieval times, and after Scandinavia adopted Christianity, central political power remained weak. Geography played an important role: The mountains of Norway and deep forests of Sweden made it difficult for any one monarch to extend his control over a large area. Traditionally, people also had the option of setting off in their ships to settle somewhere else. It was well known throughout Scandinavia that when the overbearing ruler Harold Hårfager (Harold Fairhair) threatened his subjects' right to inherit land, a group of Norwegian Viking families soon left their homes to colonize a distant, inhospitable land: Iceland.

The Icelanders passed Scandinavia's first constitution in 930, creating a system of government that has never been copied anywhere in the world. Under this document, the country was divided into four quarters and into thirty-six (later thirty-nine) districts ruled by chiefs known as *godar*. (The *godi's* traditional duty was to maintain the place of worship in his own district—a pagan temple

or simply a sacrificial rock or hill.) Each summer a national assembly, the Althing, met among the rugged cliffs and mountains of Thingvellir in southwestern Iceland. At the Althing a "lawspeaker," who was elected for a term of three years, recited the Icelandic laws from memory to the gathered citizens. Iceland's legislature is still called the Althing, although the country now also has a president, a prime minister, and rival political parties.

Viking Land-Ownership Regulation

The Althing of the Icelanders maintained many of the traditions of Viking justice, which, in turn, had grown out of ancient traditions and customs surrounding ownership of land, marriage practices, the regulation of commerce, and sanctions for violent crimes and feuds. The "legal system" of the Vikings was the collection of these traditions passed on and administered by the *thing*. Because there were no written documents, the laws were recited regularly by elder members at the *things* and in this way committed to the memories of those who attended. The Vikings had no law courts, judges, or lawyers. Each man spoke for himself before the assembly, and those who were granted a favorable judgment or punishment had the responsibility to carry out the sentence on the guilty party themselves.

In a land of limited resources, ownership of land and the traditions and laws of inheritance became the most important aspect of the unwritten laws. The Vikings closely regulated land ownership, which was considered the most important gauge of status and wealth. There were many laws and customs

Viking Politics and the Isle of Man

In Scandinavia during the Viking age, local power was commonly shared among several clans, each of which might, for example, be expected to contribute enough men to row a single warship when needed. Historian Eric Oxenstierna recounts the balance of power among the Viking settlers of the Isle of Man in *The Norsemen*.

"Most curious of all, the Isle of Man is still divided into six sheadings as it was in Viking days, when a sheading consisted of 78 families, [grouped] in 3 to form 26 *treens*. Now, according to an old Nordic conscription law, a *sheid* is the smallest warship, with 13 oars on each side, a ship with 13 benches, a 13-seater. Since 26 is the exact number required to man a 13-seater, [one out of] every three families was called upon to man a warship. The Vikings who settled on the Isle of Man therefore had to provide six such dragon ships, a fact brilliantly paralleled by the precise organization of the sheadings, and corroborated in the Middle Ages by Robert of Scotland ("the Bruce"), who, in 1313, demanded that the Isle of Man provide six ships with 26 oarsmen each.

Nowhere has the old order been so precisely preserved to the present day as on the Isle of Man, which is so small that it only had to provide 6 sheidar, or 13-seaters."

surrounding the inheritance of land; for example, members of a family generally had the first right to buy land from a kinsman who decided to sell.

There was also a system of criminal justice which covered punishments and payments for various crimes. For murder, the guilty party was supposed to make a payment (*wergild*) depending on the status of the victim (killing a thrall, for example, carried no penalty among the Vikings). Payments were also set for bodily injuries such as poking out an eye or chopping off an ear or a nose. A debtor who could not meet his obligations could be sold into slavery. For stealing, however, the guilty party would be hanged. "If they catch a thief," reported the Arab traveler Ibn Fadlan about the Rus, "they lead him to a tall, thick tree, put a sturdy rope around his neck, and hang him from the stoutest branch, leaving him dangling there until wind and rain have done their business."[24]

In some cases, an individual who defied the *thing* and its judgment was declared an outlaw. Instead of living as an outcast under these conditions, most outlaws left their homes to take their chances in a foreign land. As historian Ole Fenger explains,

In the absence of executive authority law was enforced in a negative and passive way, in which defiance or contempt of the thing meant outlawry. The outlaw had no rights, he was unable to obtain the protection of the thing, and anybody could lawfully slay him. Judgment must be backed by power, otherwise it is not judgment. All law enforcement in Scandinavia was based at this period on passive duress in the form of outlawry and deprival of rights . . . [while] law enforcement elsewhere [in Europe] was in the hands of barons, feudatories, kings or emperors.[25]

Feuds

The lack of a systematic, written set of laws among the Vikings led to a sense that justice and punishment lay mainly in the hands of the individual, the family, or the clan. A Viking readily saw his honor challenged by a neighbor or a rival, and as a result, many bloody feuds took place, sometimes lasting for generations. As Robert Wernick relates,

At any moment the daily round of farming, herding, fishing, might be torn asunder; a single spark of violence might set off an endless round of duels, ambushes, pitched battles, killings, maimings, and burnings. These blood feuds were pursued with malignant intensity, as each fresh killing stoked the furnace of hate. . . . [On Iceland] there were only two ways of settling feuds, short of the complete

William the Conqueror extended feudalism throughout Britain. By codifying laws and creating a class system based on trade, feudalism also ended clan warfare amongst the Scandinavians and incorporated them into a larger European community.

extermination of one or the other party. One was a formal reconciliation, either privately or at the Althing, with payment of *wergild,* or "blood money," for each man slain. The other was for the Althing to declare one party guilty and condemn him to an existence outside the protection of the law for a period of years or for life—"unfeedable," as the laws put it, "unfit for all help and shelter." [26]

Gradually, with contact with the rest of Europe, the system of laws and government of Scandinavia underwent important changes. Law codes were written down in a new Ro-manized alphabet, and a society of farmers saw the growth of cities and an urban class of merchants and artisans. The feuding and warring traditions of Viking kings came to an end (the successor of the Norwegian king and conqueror Harold Hardraade, who died in 1066 in England, was known as Olaf the Quiet). After his conquest of Britain, William the Conqueror forcefully introduced the feudal landownership customs of continental Europe, and Norway, Sweden, and Denmark were integrated into a much larger European system of cross-border trade. As much as the adoption of Christianity, these events brought an end to the Viking age.

Everyday Life Among the Vikings

For European historians, the Viking age officially begins with the first raids in Britain at Portland and Lindisfarne. Before this time, nearly all the people of Scandinavia lived on farms or in small farming settlements. They raised livestock and grain for their food, and used animal hides, furs, and wool for their clothing. There were few roads or bridges; travel from one isolated region to the next was difficult. Few people in Norway or Sweden ever saw or even knew about the lands beyond the ocean. A handful of people made their living by trade, and only a few outposts on the North and Baltic Seas exchanged goods with the towns of northern Europe.

By the end of the seventh century A.D., important changes were taking place in Scandinavia. As the population of Norway, Sweden, and Denmark grew, farmers found that less fertile land was available to support their families. This forced many people to abandon farming altogether and take up trade or raiding to support themselves. Another crucial development was sail power, which allowed Scandinavian ships to travel much longer distances—as far as Iceland, Greenland, North America, and the Mediterranean Sea—in search of more land and plunder.

The rest of Europe was changing as well. Arab conquerors from the Middle East were capturing Mediterranean ports and trade routes, forcing the Europeans to use more northerly routes for trade and transportation. Rivers such as the Rhine and the Seine in northern Europe became great commercial highways, linking production centers with the seas to the north and west. These new trade routes benefited the Scandinavians, who began making regular journeys to trading centers such as Dorestad on the North Sea, the main commercial center of the empire of the Franks established by Charlemagne.

In order to sell their goods to a ready market, merchants and craft workers began congregating in settlements that quickly grew into large towns. At first, traders and artisans lived in these places for short periods of time to make their articles of iron, bone, silver, and leather and sell them during seasonal fairs. Later, a permanent urban population grew as the inhabitants built sturdier homes as well as walls and fortified towers for protection.

Cities of the Viking Age

The growing Viking towns—Birka in Sweden, Ribe and Hedeby in Denmark, and Kaupang in Norway—thrived from this continental trade, even while Danish and Norwegian Vikings were attacking and pillaging cities all over Europe. The Scandinavian towns were built on important waterways and were easy to reach by ship. Other Viking towns were founded (such as Dublin, Ireland) or conquered (such as York, England) in colonies established abroad. Here the Vikings mixed with and gradually assimilated into the local population. Today, people in Britain, Normandy, Ireland, and even North Africa have Viking ancestors.

In many ways, the new Viking towns were similar to those in the rest of northern Europe at this time. There was no planning or surveying; the houses rose helter-skelter along unpaved paths or streets paved with wooden planks. A hill or a grove of trees might hold a temple to a patron god such as Frey or Thor. Protective walls of staves (poles or planks) and stones surrounded farming estates, and town defenses were also carefully planned. Historian Gwyn Jones notes that "even as the merchant ship or ferry carried arms, so the towns between which they plied were protected by being sited away from the sea, inside narrow fjords like Hedeby and Lindholm Hoje, on inland lakes like Birka and Sigtuna, on rivers leading from such lakes like Aldeigjuborg, Old Ladoga, or within bays where islands, shoals, and complicated channels made the approach slow and observable. . . . In addition many of the towns were given strong man-made defenses, like the northern fort and look-out station and the semicircular rampart at Hedeby, the rock-fortress and town wall of Birka, and the earthwork stronghold of Grobin." [27]

Houses were built close to a source of fresh water, either a stream or a lake; wells were dug and reinforced with heavy stones or with staves. There were no sewers, and each

The Mysterious Ring Forts of the Danes

The largest monuments left behind by the pre-Christian Scandinavian people are not buried ships, great pagan temples, or colossal picture stones, but instead walls of earth and stone surrounding the four "ring forts" that were left behind by the kings of Denmark about one thousand years ago.

The huge walls of these forts are precisely circular, as if they had been carefully drawn on a blueprint with a compass and pen. They stand between 10 and 15 feet high and as much as 60 feet thick at Trelleborg, Fyrkat, Nonnebajjen, and Aggersborg (the largest of the ring forts at 787 feet in diameter). The forts show signs of careful design and construction. Within the walls were two ruler-straight main streets, paved with wooden planks and laid out at right angles. The streets divided the forts into four equal quadrants and ended at four gates cut into the earthen walls. In each quadrant longhouses were raised in groups of four, each group surrounding a courtyard. At Trelleborg the side walls curved outward, giving the buildings a nautical shape. Workshops, stables, and living quarters were set up in each quadrant. Altogether the four ring forts could house as many as 6,000 soldiers—a huge army for that time in Europe.

The precise, regular design of the Danish ring forts show that they were probably used as military posts or barracks. Yet they still hold their mysteries. Historians do not know who built the forts or why. They may have been staging posts for raids on England or Norway or protected barracks built to house an army of foreign mercenaries. Strangely, at Trelleborg, archaeologists have found axes, spears, and arrow points, but not a single sword—the most common weapon of the Viking age. Also, these sites hold many female as well as male skeletons.

Excavations have turned up little: foundations, postholes, and a few graves and artifacts. Otherwise, the walls of the ring forts stand massive and silent, guarding mysteries about the Vikings of Denmark that may never be solved.

A reconstruction of a Viking village. The houses are made of timber and roofed with twigs and grasses.

house had its own rubbish heap. The larger towns manufactured their own goods in smithies, pottery works, ironworks, shipyards, glassworks, and tanneries.

Late in the Viking age, as power became more centralized, the Viking towns became large, affluent cities. Hedeby, the largest metropolis of the Viking era, covered about sixty acres and at its height held a population of several thousand people. The increasingly powerful kings established royal residences in the towns; their armies protected the traders from raiding and granted trading rights that helped the permanent population of merchants to grow wealthier. With the conversion of Scandinavia to Christianity, churches and bishoprics were also established, which in turn promoted scholarly and literary pursuits. These activities gave the towns increasing importance in the cultural life of the new Scandinavian kingdoms.

Building a Home

Before the growth of towns, however, the Vikings were farmers, hunters, traders, and warriors. They lived and worked outdoors,

tilling and planting the fields they owned, hunting or gathering food in the forests, or traveling from one village or region to the next. In seasons of fair weather, they took to their ships to journey across the seas to trade with or attack distant places in Britain or the continent of Europe.

To a Viking, home was a place to sleep or eat, a hall to feast in during celebrations, and, usually, a safe place to keep possessions and valuables. Their houses were small, and most of them had only a single room. They might be built of stone, of turf cut from the surrounding fields, or of heavy tree branches plastered with mud. Some Viking houses had walls formed by rows of stone alternating with turf. The foundations and lower walls of several of these houses survive in the abandoned Viking colonies of Vestribygth (Western Settlement) and Eystribygth (Eastern Settlement) in Greenland.

Available materials depended on the location. Few trees grow on Iceland, the Shetland and Orkney Islands, or in northern Britain. In these places the Vikings used stone cut from cliffsides, mountains, and quarries. In Norway, Sweden, and Denmark, forests of oak, birch, and pine provided timber for houses,

The location of a settlement determined what building materials were available. When wood was scarce, the Vikings used stone and sod to construct their homes.

outbuildings, workshops, and barns. In some places, building materials changed and improved over time. Viking historian Magnus Magnusson notes the improvements made at the Viking settlement in the Coppergate neighborhood of York: "The earliest Viking settlers in Coppergate built houses of wattle-and-post—twigs and withies woven around posts driven into the ground and daubed with clay to make them weatherproof. But the next generation built in a much more substantial fashion: walls constructed of solid oaken planks laid horizontally on thick foundation beams, supported by squared internal uprights, with a roof of wooden shingles. These Coppergate houses, set end-on to the street-front, were the first well-preserved Viking timber buildings ever found in Britain."[28]

To raise a new house, builders fashioned straight and heavy oak posts and planted them in deep postholes to serve as roof supports. Walls of pine staves were placed vertically in the ground, lashed to the posts, and plastered with a mixture of mud, straw, and animal dung. The Vikings also built walls of horizontal logs, notched at the ends, or fashioned a lattice of tree branches (wattle), which was then plastered with mud and straw (daub). To allow light from the outside, some Viking homes had small windows made of thin, translucent animal membranes.

The Great Hoards of the Vikings

Modern Scandinavia is a land of buried treasures—hundreds of them. In places where the land has long been settled, farmers, children, laborers, and even dogs have turned up old clay pots or small caskets that were buried and then forgotten during Viking times. These long-lost hoards carry useful clues about the society and the economy of Scandinavia during the Viking age.

In times of trouble, the Vikings buried their valuables in fields, quarries, or mounds—wherever their owners were certain they would not be found. The hoards contained jewelry, coins, and silver in the form of broken fragments ("hack" silver) that was traded by its weight. Many of the hoards contained silver coins from the Middle East, also known as Kufic coins after the Kufic lettering stamped on them. Kufic coins always carried the year they were produced; some also showed the place they were made. By dating the latest such coin in a hoard, modern archaeologists can determine the earliest date the hoard could have been buried and can make a rough guess of the year when it was assembled.

Dating all the hoards in a certain region also gives historians an idea of when, in general, invasions and civil disturbances were occurring. Numerous hoards from a certain period reveal troubles. For example, the number of hoards in England from the years 1065–1070, the years of the bloody Norman Conquest, is more than that of the five decades before. In Norway there are many hoards from the troubled time of St. Olaf, who died in battle in 1030, but few from the time of Magnus the Good, who reigned peacefully from 1035 until 1047.

More than half of all the hoards in Scandinavia have been discovered on the island of Gotland, which lies off the coast of Sweden in the Baltic Sea. More than ninety thousand silver coins were unearthed before 1946—and these represented only those forgotten or left behind by their owners. These hoards demonstrate that Gotland's location, between Scandinavia and the Russian trade routes that led to the Middle East, allowed the island to become the wealthiest place in the Viking world.

Treasure from a Viking burial hoard. These coins were plundered from the Byzantine Empire and various Islamic kingdoms.

For the roof, blocks of turf or a blanket of reeds and thatch were laid over a planking of birch bark, which served to keep out rain and snow. (To support the heavy roof, stone walls had to be as much as two yards thick). A hole cut in the center of the roof allowed smoke from the hearth to escape. In places where inside support posts were not used, wooden poles were sometimes placed along the outside walls to keep the house from sagging underneath the weight of the roof.

The Vikings dug some of their houses out of the ground, so that the interior floor lay below ground level. This construction allowed the surrounding earth to insulate the home. But in a heavy storm, such a building would easily flood with water and mud. Thus, sunken-floored buildings were most often used as sheds, as smithies, or as living quarters for slaves.

Within the Walls

The floor plan of the Viking home was simple: Most had only a single long, rectangular room. Loose straw covered the earth floor, and in some homes, woven tapestries hung on the walls and helped to keep the house warm. Along the walls were low wooden benches or banks of earth for sitting, dining, and for sleeping. Larger Viking homes (or "longhouses") had a central "great hall" and several smaller rooms that led off the main room.

Most Viking homes were sparsely furnished with a few stools, small tables, and storage chests. The chests were used to hold clothing, shoes, furs, tools, jewelry, and other personal belongings. In times of feuding or civil war, the chests could be moved outdoors to a safe underground hiding place. Wealthy families furnished their homes with glass drinking cups, wooden beds and chairs, and vessels of silver and gold.

The center of every Viking home was the hearth, which was dug out of the center of the main room. The hearth provided light, heat, and a cooking fire. Within the hearth stood a spit for roasting meat as well as cauldrons for cooking porridges and stews. Cooking pots hung from chains suspended from the ceiling. Near the hearth lay iron skillets and ladles, buckets for milk, butter, or cheese, and clay plates and bowls. For light, the Vikings used

The rather spartan furnishings of a typical Viking home are exemplified in this reconstruction.

stone or clay lamps that burned whale or seal oil. By the tenth century, the Vikings began using wax candles, which arrived from the European continent. A Viking home must have smelled of wood smoke and damp earth, of burning seal oil, of the bread, ale, and roasting meat served around the hearth, and, in winter, the livestock that farmers brought inside to share the shelter and warmth of the house.

Food

A fire was always burning in the hearth of a Viking house, sparked by striking steel against flint or quartz and fueled by branches, bark, logs, or, in areas of few trees, by smoking peat or turf. Here, Viking families prepared their two meals of the day: one in the morning (*dagverthar*) and one in the evening (*nattverthar*). The evening meal, the heartiest of the day, was served after sundown, when work stopped in the surrounding fields and hunters came in with their prey.

Viking cooks prepared their main meals in cauldrons or cooking pans placed over the hearth. Meat or fish were prepared in small pots, or wrapped in leaves, and then placed in the ground with heated stones for cooking. Meat could also be boiled in pots with vegetables or roasted on spits over an open fire. To eat, the Vikings used clay or wooden plates, bowls, and cups, as well as knives and spoons; forks were still unknown.

As in the rest of Europe, bread was the staple food of Scandinavia. The Vikings made their bread from ground rye or barley flour; finer wheat flour was uncommon. Large, heavy stones, known as querns, were used to grind the grain into flour; fragments from the querns often mixed with the flour, making it gritty. The dough was rolled out and then baked over an open fire or placed on a cook-ing pan among the hot ashes. The Vikings did not use leavening; the bread had to be eaten quickly before it hardened. When grain was short, cooks extended their dough by using ground, dried peas or the inner layers of pine bark.

Cabbage, peas, and onions were the most common vegetables, cooked in stews with a mixture of herbs as well as beef, pork, or fish (fish replaced meat as the main source of protein in Viking towns). For meat, the Vikings raised cattle, pigs, and sheep; they also hunted the abundant boar, elk, deer, and bear in the Scandinavian forests. In lands too cold or infertile for crops, hunting replaced farming. On the barren coasts of Greenland, the Viking colonists depended on seal, fox, marten, reindeer, polar bear, and arctic caribou. In addition, the Vikings ate whale and seal meat as well as game birds, honey, eggs, and wild fruits such as apples, plums, and berries.

Before the cold winters began, it was common for Viking families to slaughter their weak or old livestock, smoke the meat, and then pickle it in salt gathered from seaweed or seawater to preserve it. Fish was dried by hanging outside in the open air, then pickled in saltwater or smoked in a shed. Harvested vegetables and grain were stored in small adjoining rooms or in nearby sheds. In times of food shortages or famine, the Vikings had to survive on tree bark, wild nuts, and seaweed. On their long sea voyages, the Vikings stocked their ships with salted meat and fish, water, milk, and beer.

The Vikings brewed beer and also prepared mead, a strong, sweet fermented drink made from honey. Wine from the Rhineland area of Germany was rare and too expensive for anyone but the wealthiest chieftains and kings. Yet Vikings did not have to be royalty in order to be treated well in each other's homes. When guests arrived after a long journey, the best food was always brought out. The Viking poem *Havamal* advises its listeners: "When a guest arrives chilled to the very knees from his journey through the mountains, he needs fire, food, and dry clothes."[29]

Clothing

Unlike bones, silver, or iron, wool and leather usually can not survive one thousand years of burial underground. For this reason, discoveries of original Viking clothing are very rare and survive only as small fragments. To describe the Viking wardrobe, historians must use these rare finds as well as illustrations made on jewelry, tapestries, picture stones, or wood carvings.

It seems, from this evidence, that the main item worn by the Vikings was a long cloak fastened at the shoulders. It was common for Viking men to wear their cloak thrown over one shoulder to keep their right arm free to carry and wield a weapon. Cloaks might be trimmed with fur and decorated with embroidery; they were held in place by open clasps for men or closed oval brooches for women. The pagan Vikings buried their dead fully dressed, and for this reason these metal brooches have become one of the most common objects found in their graves. Wealthy Vikings wore brooches made of silver or gold, carefully worked by skilled jewelers and richly decorated; others wore plain bronze or tin brooches, manufactured by the hundreds out of common soapstone molds.

Underneath the cloak Viking men also wore leather belts and jackets as well as baggy trousers that were gathered at the knee. Women wore linen shirts and long woolen dresses, some of them without sleeves. The wealthier Vikings could afford silk clothing imported from Byzantium and the Middle East. They decorated themselves with ribbons and pleated cords, and their clothing with intricate embroidery. As in Europe, caps were worn by the Scandinavians and made of leather, wool, or silk, and they were sometimes decorated with small tassels.

Viking shoes were made of calfskin or goatskin and were commonly laced around the ankle. The Vikings used skates or iron spikes for walking across the winter ice. Ice skates were made from the long bones of horses' feet, smoothed out with a plane and lashed to the shoes. Skis were used for transportation over snowbound trails while hunting, trapping, or

Viking Fashion at Herjolfsnes

In one excavation at Herjolfsnes, on the southern tip of Greenland, archaeologists discovered several skeletons still wearing their burial clothing, preserved for more than five hundred years by the frozen ground. Found in the graves were several woolen robes and dresses with rounded necklines. Also scattered among the bodies were liripipe hoods, a high fashion item in the Middle Ages. These caps covered the head, neck, and shoulders and sported a long, thin tassel that hung down from the back of the head.

The clothing found at Herjolfsnes shows that the Greenlanders preferred the fashions of Europe to the warmer, more practical clothing made of skins and furs worn by the native Inuit. The many patches and wear and tear in the clothing also show that the Greenlanders endured a hard poverty that eventually brought European settlement of the region to an end.

A fanciful woodcut of a Viking displays the intricate clothing and accoutrements that were common to warriors. The well-crafted metalwork and woven cords, however, indicate that this was probably a man of wealth.

trading. The people of Scandinavia had already been skiing for a long time; the oldest skis ever found—the Kalvtrask skis of Sweden—are more than five thousand years old.

Everyday Weapons

All Vikings—men and women, traders, merchants, craftsmen, warriors, and pirates—owned and carried weapons. A long sword, usually made of iron and double-edged, hung from a Viking's belt and was considered his single most important possession. The grips and hilts of the swords were sometimes finely worked; the blade might carry a runic inscription that identified its owner. The best swords of the Viking age came from the Frankish Empire. They were so superior that both Charlemagne and Charles the Bald forbade Frankish

This highly detailed Viking brooch exhibits delicate enamel work and is dotted with precious stones.

smiths from exporting them, threatening death to any smith who disobeyed their orders.

In battle the Vikings also used spears, axes, and bows and arrows. For protection they carried a wooden shield with a central iron boss; better-equipped warriors used a heavy suit of chain mail, which was made up of hundreds of small, forged iron links. Helmets were worn to protect the head, made of either leather or of much sturdier iron. Men also carried knives on their belts, while women carried smaller knives, keys, and small domestic tools such as scissors and needles on chains or in small boxes. In areas where iron was scarce, such as Greenland, weapons were made of whalebone or seal bone. Arrowheads and spear points made from the antlers of reindeer have also been found in the far north.

Looking at the Vikings

Many foreigners who met the Vikings were impressed with their appearance. The Arab writer Ibn Fadlan, who met a colony of Swedish Vikings in Russia, was quoted by Eric Oxenstierna in *The Norsemen* as saying, "I have never seen humans more nobly built. They are tall as palm trees, red blond, with light skins. They wear neither shirt nor coat with sleeves. From the tips of their nails to their necks these men are tattooed with trees and various figures."

From analyzing skeletal remains in Norway and Denmark, archaeologists can tell much about the Vikings' appearance (in Sweden bodies were usually cremated). Viking adult men averaged 5 feet 6 inches; women about 5 feet 2 inches. On average they had fairly long skulls, narrow noses, and rectangular eye sockets. Their hard physical labor often caused arthritis; their teeth were ground down by the coarse bread they ate.

In the poor settlements of Greenland, skeletons showed signs of rickets, tuberculosis, and deformed spines. Portraits of the Vikings on jewelry and stones show that men usually wore beards and mustaches.

Visitors to the Viking town of Hedeby noticed that both women and men used cosmetics. Ibn Fadlan, however, was not impressed by the hygiene of the Swedish Vikings he encountered. "They are the filthiest of God's creatures. They do not wash after discharging their natural functions, neither do they wash their hands after meals. Every day they wash their faces and heads, all using the same water which is as filthy as can be imagined." Articles of personal hygiene were more common among wealthy Viking families, whose graves held combs made of bone or of antler, wash basins, tweezers, and special scrapers for cleaning out the ears.

An Icelandic chieftain falls to the swing of a Viking longsword. This double-edged blade was a Norseman's most important possession.

Sports and Games

The Vikings may have spent many of their long, dark, winter evenings telling traditional stories and playing familiar games. Small gaming pieces of wood, stone, walrus ivory, bone, and amber have been found in graves and in homesites throughout the Viking world. One board game of the Vikings was *hneftafl*. In this game players maneuver a set of pieces around a square board in an attempt to defend or capture a king. One *hneftafl* board was found in Ireland. The board contains forty-nine small peg holes to hold the pieces for each side and a central hole for the king piece. By the eleventh century, or the end of the Viking age, the game of chess had arrived in northern Europe from India and the Middle East.

Viking children had their own games and toys. Archaeologists have discovered small wooden models of horses, for example, and miniature tools with which Viking children began the toil of farming at an early age. Small wooden toy boats have also been found at many seaside excavations.

As grown-ups, the Vikings took the greatest delight in matches of strength and endurance. According to Icelandic sagas, they sometimes played war games and conducted contests of physical strength, including wrestling and rowing matches. One popular summer sport among the Vikings was stallion fighting. "There were many stallions, everybody had a good time, and the contests were fairly even," reports the *Viga-Glums Saga*. "Many stallion fights took place on this day. In the end it came about that an equal number of stallions had bitten well on both sides, and an equal number had run away."[30] The stallion bouts often took place during the annual horse festivals of early autumn, which survive in Scandinavia as yearly horse fairs in certain towns.

CHAPTER 5

Farmers, Builders, and Traders

Although they are best remembered as warriors and sailors, most Scandinavians of the Viking age were farmers who rarely traveled away from their homes. They built their own houses, tools, and ships, and forged their own weapons. Instead of an economy similar to modern Europe, the Vikings used a system of barter in which goods are traded for other goods. The barter system, and the problems that prevented transporting crops and goods over long distances, forced each individual to be as self-sufficient as possible.

With contact with the rest of Europe, however, the Viking "economy" began to change. Trading centers were set up in towns such as Birka and Hedeby, where merchants from distant lands arrived to buy and sell Viking goods, especially furs. In Hedeby, the first Viking coins were minted and exchanged, and a system of money began to replace the barter of earlier times. Scandinavia joined the larger European trading network as the Viking raids came to an end, the people of Norway, Sweden, and Denmark accepted Christianity, and the first large manufacturing centers grew along waterways that had once seen only the passing vessels of pirates and raiders.

Scarce Land and Cold Weather

The main problem facing all Viking farmers was a scarcity of arable land, which was distributed unevenly throughout Scandinavia.

Only a narrow strip along the seacoast serves as suitable cropland in Norway. (Although winters were harsh in Norway, the warm Gulf Stream current brings mild temperatures in spring and summer to the coast.) Sweden was, and still is, covered with dense forests and long chains of lakes, while land in much of Denmark is sandy or boggy. Adam of Bremen, a German cleric who traveled in these parts during the Viking age, reported that

> whilst the whole land of Germany is frightful with thick forests, Jutland [the main peninsula of Denmark] is still more frightful, where the land is shunned on account of the poverty of its produce and the sea on account of the infestation of pirates. Cultivation is found hardly anywhere, hardly any place exists suitable for human habitation, but wherever there are arms of the sea, there the country has very large settlements.[31]

Iceland has almost no land suitable for growing crops; Viking farmers there raised sheep and depended on fish and birds for their food supply. But the Viking settlers to the northwest in Greenland had it even worse. Despite its name, which was created as a propaganda ploy by the Norwegian explorer Erik the Red to attract settlers, Greenland had a growing season much too short for food crops. The Greenlanders had to rely on livestock and especially hunting and fishing to support themselves. Trade from the outside

The first Vikings arrive in Greenland. Because the land was unsuitable for crops, the Greenland settlements died out after cargo ships failed to keep the settlers supplied.

was crucial; later, when the climate of the northern hemisphere turned colder, cargo ships from Europe stopped arriving in Greenland, and the isolated settlements died out.

Farm Work

The farmers' hardest task was preparing a new field for cultivation, since this involved clearing the land of both stones and trees. To break and turn the soil, farmers used an *ard,* an iron-bladed plow, pulled by horses or oxen. Tree roots had to be removed and heavy rocks lifted and carried out of the way. It was customary for farmers to pile up these stones to make cairns on hilltops, many of which still stand today.

Viking farmers planted and harvested their land with the members of their immediate family. Some also had the services of slaves, brought from Europe on raids and sold or traded for goods in Scandinavia. Small smithies were built on the property to make the necessary tools. To supplement crops and livestock raised on the farm, the Vikings often hunted, fished, or left on raiding expeditions when the winds were right.

The principal crops of the Vikings were grains: wheat, barley, and rye. The grain was harvested with sharp iron scythes or sickles, allowed to dry, then gathered and ground with heavy querns. As fertilizer, farmers used cow dung. In some places, a system of crop rotation was used, with fields planted with grain one year, vegetables the next. Viking farms were carefully laid out and usually included a shed or byre to shelter the horses, oxen, cows, sheeps, and pigs that were raised for food or used as work animals. The livestock grazed on nearby pastures, but when nearby pasture land became scarce, the animals were driven to summer pastures at higher altitudes.

Manufacturing

Well before the Vikings, the Iron Age had arrived in Scandinavia when the people of the region learned to mine local iron ore (called "bog iron" because much of it was found in marshy land). To extract raw, usable iron from the ore, they built small stone cauldrons directly over the ore-bearing earth and placed burning charcoal within the cauldrons. A bellows pumped air into the side of the cauldron, keeping the fire going until it reached a temperature of about a thousand degrees. As the ore slowly melted, forming slag, a small

"bloom" of iron was formed at the bottom of the cauldron. The iron bloom was then removed from the cauldron and, in the form of small slabs or bars, worked into tools and weapon blades.

The best iron ore of Viking times came from southern Sweden, which carried on a profitable trade in ore with Germany. Eventually, small iron production centers grew up in more populated regions. On the Oslo fjord in Norway, the settlement of Kaupang contained iron and bronze workshops and traded with the mainland of Europe. Ribe in Denmark and Helgo on Lake Mälaren in Sweden produced bronze and iron goods for export. The search for suitable ore led to further colonization of unknown areas of Scandinavia itself, as historian Gert Magnusson explains:

> In the early Iron Age, most iron-production sites must have been near permanent settlements. The amount of slag found shows that production was very limited and mainly designed to fulfill the needs of a

The Archaeology of Farming

In his book *The Vikings,* historian Holger Arbman describes the discovery of a Viking era field in Denmark, preserved just as it was a millennium ago by a sudden sandstorm.

"Outside Aalborg in Denmark . . . part of a village and its grave field have been cleared. It was crowded within a wooden palisade, and its burial field lay outside this on a mound. . . . At the end of the tenth century the site was buried by a sand-drift as decisively as Pompeii by its lava, and has been undisturbed since then. When the sand was removed, the cemetery was revealed exact-

ly as it was in the tenth century with the stones arranged in various figures, triangles, circles and squares; no vegetation had grown over them, and not a stone had been moved. The ploughed fields ran right up to the cemetery and one can still see the long narrow high-backed strips produced by ploughing towards the center to make the land corrugated and self-draining; perhaps the sand came in the autumn after the ploughing. There was a road along the field, rather narrow, and one can see where a two-wheeled cart drove out over the furrows just before the storm."

farm or village. . . . The limited local resources were incapable of increasing production unless the ironworkers became colonizers and exploiters of wastelands, such as the mountain valleys and plateaux of south Norway or the forests of Dalarna, Halsingland, Gastrikland and Smaland in Sweden.[32]

Many Viking farms had their own small iron-making operations and smithies, used to provide needed implements as well as the double-edged swords, axes, and spears used for raiding and for defense. Historian James Graham-Campbell explains:

Viking smithies turned out fine products crafted from iron and bronze. Items like this helmet were used by the Vikings, but they were also exported to other parts of Europe.

Such smithies would have to have been provided with a basic tool kit, including bellows and protective furnace stone; tongs and hammers were needed for handling and shaping the hot iron, with an anvil to beat it upon. Shears were required for cutting sheet metal. Chisels and files were essential, and nail-making was done with a special perforated iron tool to help finish the head.[33]

A Silver Age

The metal most prized by the Vikings was not iron but silver, yet Scandinavia holds no silver deposits. Silver had to be imported into the region, either by piracy, by trade, or in the form of huge ransom payments made by European realms held hostage by Viking raiders. Much silver arrived in the form of Arabic coins known as dirhams. Eventually so much foreign silver was arriving in Scandinavia that it became a basic medium of exchange. Instead of coins or notes, the Vikings paid each other in the form of silver that was cut into fragments and weighed out on small scales. Many hoards from the Viking era contain large quantities of this "hack" silver.

To a Viking farmer or landowner, the buried hoard, with its jewelry, Arabic coins, and hack silver, served as the family bank account. Hundreds of such hoards, forgotten during a conflict or after the death of their owners, have been dug up by modern Scandinavian archaeologists and farmers. The largest such hoard was found at Cuerdale in Lancashire, England. Dating to around 900, the hoard contained jewelry, hack silver, and seven thousand coins, weighing a total of eighty-eight pounds.

A finely wrought silver armband. Since Scandinavia has no silver deposits, Viking silversmiths melted down looted silver coins to fashion their wares.

Smithies and Workshops

Workshops for the manufacture of household tools and jewelry to be used as trade items were built in Viking towns such as Helgo and Birka in Sweden and Hedeby in Denmark. The smiths melted ingots or scraps of metal in a clay crucible that was heated over a charcoal fire. The molten metal was then poured through a small opening into a clay or soapstone mold, in which a design had been carved by hand or impressed on the inner surface with a finished object. Viking craftsmen also employed the lost-wax process, creating wax models of objects, covering the models with clay, and then letting the clay dry and harden. When heated, the wax melted and flowed out of the mold, leaving a cavity that could then be filled with molten metal. When the metal cooled and hardened, the clay mold was then broken away from it.

To make a bowl or drinking cup, the Viking smith hammered out the desired shape from a flat sheet of metal. Silver ingots could also be hammered into armbands or pendants; thin rods of metal could be plaited into finger rings. To decorate their objects, Viking smiths used long rods known as punches, which carried a small design at their ends that could be stamped into a metal surface to create an intricate pattern. Silver could also be hammered directly onto the surface of iron sheet metal to give it a polished sheen. Small rods of silver were sometimes inlaid into the hilt of a sword handle or the top of a brooch in an intricate pattern previously engraved in the surface. Fine wires of silver and gold were used in filigreed works in which they were soldered to a metal surface. Often silver was combined with

Greenland Goods

In Greenland, a place with no trees or iron deposits, one of the most useful raw materials was ivory from the tusks of walrus and narwhal. Hunters sailed north along the western coast of Greenland to find and harvest the tusks; the Greenlanders also may have traded for tusks with the Inuit. Walrus ivory was useful for making combs, pins, and jewelry inlay; it also could be traded with more fertile countries such as Norway for grain and clothing.

After the end of the Viking age, walrus ivory remained the Greenlanders' most valuable trading item. In 1327 the representative of the pope, the leader of the Catholic Church, arrived in Greenland and collected 250 tusks as a church tithe. But soon afterward, a migration of Inuit took place southward along Greenland's western coast. Scandinavian settlers had to give up walrus hunting and abandon their Western Settlement. The end of the walrus trade, and the loss of valuable pasture land for their livestock, brought about the end of the Greenland colonies.

other metals, such as tin, copper, bronze, and gold, to provide a contrast of texture and color.

Much manufacturing in Viking times was done by transient craftsmen rather than by masters or apprentices in workshops. Skilled artisans traveled from village to village, making and selling useful goods such as knives, keys, and other household items. The traveling chest of one such smith was found buried at the bottom of Lake Mastermyr in Sweden in 1936. The chest contained tools for pounding out kettles; making barrels, nails, and cow bells; repairing iron goods; cutting, chiseling, and planing wood; and working on boats. The chest also contained sets of scales; the smith probably sold the goods he made by weight.

Trade

The Vikings were not the first people of Scandinavia to trade their goods with the European continent. During the time of the Roman Empire, cargo ships from the north called on ports along the Baltic and the North Seas, bringing amber, slaves, and thick fur pelts. The northerners traded their goods for Roman glass, bronze ornaments, tableware, cloth, and jewelry.

The migrations that brought about the collapse of the Western Roman Empire in the fifth century temporarily interrupted this trade. Eventually, trade was resumed with small kingdoms and principalities founded in northern Europe and Great Britain in the seventh century. New trade routes crisscrossed the North Sea, from Norway and Denmark to the coast of Europe and eastern Great Britain.

A new class of professional, full-time Scandinavian traders took advantage of these routes. Many of these merchants had no home; they sailed or wandered overland constantly, buying and selling wherever they could. They brought their goods south to Dorestad and other trading ports on the North and Baltic seacoasts, where buyers sought

A selection of molds used to fashion tools and jewelry. Molten metal was poured into these molds and then when the metal cooled, the molds would be broken away to reveal the finished items.

Merchants of the Rus

In his book AD 1000: Living on the Brink of Apocalypse, historian Richard Erdoes quotes the Arab traveler Ibn Fadlan, who wrote about the business practices of the Rus he met in what is now Russia.

"As soon as their ships reach the main anchorage, every one of these fellows goes on land, well-provided with bread, meat, onions, milk, and intoxicating drinks. He walks over to a huge pole the top of which is carved in the likeness of a human face. This big image is surrounded by a number of smaller idols. He walks up to the big one, bows down, and address it: 'O my Lord! I have come from a far country and have so and so many girls with me, and so and so many sable or marten pelts.' And he goes 'My Lord, a gift,' and he lays his presents at the foot of the pole and says: 'I want thee to send me a buyer with many coins of gold and silver, who takes all my goods without haggling.' Then he walks away. If business is bad, and he has to tarry longer than he wants, he goes back, bringing more presents to the big pole, and if this doesn't help, he gives presents to the smaller idols, saying: 'These are my Lord's sons and daughters whom I ask to come to my aid.'

But if business is good and he sells all his merchandise at a great profit, he says, 'My Lord has fulfilled all that I asked for, it is my duty to repay him.' He then takes a number of oxen and sheep, slaughters them, gives some of the meat to the poor, hanging the head and some meat of the oxen around the neck of the big pole, and the head of the sheep and some mutton meat on the smaller ones. During the night come the dogs and eat it all. Then the fellow says happily: 'My Lord loves me. He has consumed my gifts.'"

Scandinavian furs, reputed to be the best in Europe, as well as walrus tusks, amber, beeswax, honey, hunting falcons, and slaves.

The traders brought back goods from Europe that were in high demand in Scandinavia. These included swords from the Frankish Empire, cloth from England, and wine from the Rhineland. Within Scandinavia, Viking farmers and artisans regularly traded their goods for articles they could not obtain nearby, such as raw iron in the form of bars, soapstone to be used for jewelry molds, and whetstones for sharpening tools. The people of Greenland, unable to raise crops for food, traded sealskins, walrus ivory, and the skins of polar bears for grain from Norway, livestock from Iceland, and useful tools they could not make themselves.

Hedeby and Ribe in Denmark, Helgo and Birka in Sweden, and Kaupang in Norway became the largest Viking trading centers. At these places, merchants brought their goods to annual or seasonal fairs, where they sold to buyers who came from other Viking lands, from northern Europe, or from Russia. The fairs often took place during the winter, when fur pelts were at their thickest and northern marshes and streams could be more easily crossed by sled and by ski.

The First Viking Money

Ribe and the other trading centers eventually grew into manufacturing centers in their own right. Eventually, in the tenth century, the people of Hedeby began minting their own coins—the first in the Viking world. These Hedeby "half-bracteates" were small, thin silver coins that carried only a single stamp, usually a design of an animal or a ship, on both sides (the coins were never dated). As an increasing number of the Hedeby coins were manufactured and used in trading, they gradually spread across Denmark and up the major commercial rivers of Germany.

The evidence for the introduction of coinage in the Viking world comes not from documents or eyewitness accounts, but from the earth. Archaeologists digging in Hedeby have found soapstone molds used for making silver bars in layers that date back to the year 950; in higher strata, or layers of the site, the finds date from a later time, and no such soapstone molds were found. As historian Eric Oxenstierna explains,

> Haithabu [Hedeby] had gone over to a purely coin currency; no other kind was permitted.

The reason is simple. On arrival, traders had to exchange their hack silver and for-

---

The End of Hedeby

The people of Hedeby might have been the wealthiest commoners of the entire Viking age. They made a wide variety of goods to sell: ships, iron tools, woven textiles, jewelry, and chain mail. They also collected tolls from passing ships, as the town lay on an important portage between the North and Baltic Seas that allowed sailors to cross the Danish peninsula safely, without having to sail the rough and dangerous seas around the northern tip of Denmark.

Although it thrived from peaceful manufacturing and trade, Hedeby was eventually caught up in the long-standing rivalry between the kings of Denmark and Norway. Historian Johannes Brondsted recounts the legend of Hedeby's destruction in *The Vikings*.

"History testifies very plainly to the situation which arose in the middle of eleventh century, when King Swein Estridsson of Denmark and King Harald Hadrada of Norway came to grips with each other. About 1050, Harald seized the opportunity to fall upon Hedeby, plundering and burning it to the ground. As Swein, returning from the south, approached the place, Harald's ships, loaded with loot, made off. Swein pursued him and caught up with him at Laeso in the Kattegat, where Harald, to lighten his vessels and escape, was forced to throw his rich Hedeby plunder overboard—so that it floated on the wind-swept Jutland sea, as the skald Thorleik the Fair says in his song. Another skald, a Norwegian who was with King Harald, celebrated the fate of Hedeby in jubilant song: 'Burnt in anger was Hedeby from end to end. It was a doughty deed and one from which Swein [of Denmark] will smart. High rose the flames from the houses when, last night before dawn, I stood on the stronghold's arm.'"

Archaeologists excavating the site of Hedeby have found strong evidence for the city's catastrophic end: a thick layer of charcoal and ash at the uppermost layer of the soil, where the burnt remains of houses and objects date to around the middle of the eleventh century.

When the Vikings began minting coins, the designs were simple. These early coins bear some of the crude images.

eign coins for the local currency, which gave the issuer the chance, in the course of melting down and casting, to keep an appropriate amount of the "scrap" metal for himself. This was "tribute" that he had coming to him as his own personal tax levy. The local rulers in Germany and France were doing the same thing. What we witness here is a giant step toward a monetary standard.[34]

At the same time, the flow of Arabic coins brought north from countless trading expeditions to the Middle East began to dry up. The silver mines of the Middle East were exhausted; Viking traders and merchants turned to a much closer source of money and goods: Germany. European merchants now paid for Scandinavian furs with silver produced by mines in the Harz Mountains of Germany. This practice, among others, slowly integrated Denmark and the rest of Scandinavia into the larger European trading system, an event that was hurried by the end of the Viking raids and the conversion of Scandinavia to Christianity.

CHAPTER 6

Viking Language, Art, and Poetry

The artists and poets of the Viking age are silent about their works. They left no books or essays behind to express their ideas; they gave no interviews to roaming scribes of the Dark Ages. Similarly, Scandinavian artists did not begin signing their works until the eleventh century, when the era of the Vikings was nearly past.

There is no doubt that skilled artists lived among the Vikings. Nearly every large artifact ever discovered in Viking graves and in the ruins of Viking settlements carries some kind of elaborate decoration. Some are simple and crude, while others are hypnotically complex. From the few lines of their works that survive, Viking poets also show a taste for the difficult and the complex, using a tangled code of symbols and metaphors that in some works still defies understanding. At a time when Christian themes and ideas held sway in neighboring lands, these Viking jewelers, smiths, stone carvers, and poets were creating the final works of a pagan, polytheistic art that had its origins in prehistoric Europe.

The Viking Tongue

The Scandinavians of the Viking era spoke their own version of the Germanic languages of northern Europe. A distinct Scandinavian branch of the Germanic language developed by the sixth century, well before the first Viking raids in the eighth century. This "Old Norse" or "Common Scandinavian" language was spo-ken in Norway, Denmark, Sweden, Iceland, and the Faeroe, Shetland, and Orkney Islands. Eventually, two main branches of Old Norse developed, known as East Norse and West Norse. Shortly after the end of the Viking age, the local dialects of East Norse began developing into modern Danish and Swedish; West Norse became Norwegian and Icelandic (modern Icelandic being the language closest to Old Norse in its grammar and vocabulary).

To the people of Great Britain and Europe, all Vikings spoke "Danish." Like Old English, Old Norse was a grammatically complicated language. Its nouns and adjectives were inflected, meaning they had various endings which indicated their gender (male or female) and case (object, direct object, etc.). Verbs had a certain tense as well as a certain number, person, and mood. The people of England may have noticed that the language spoken by the Danes was closely related to their own language, which also belongs to the Germanic group of Indo-European languages. In fact, the English and Danish probably were able to communicate with each other while still speaking their native tongues. Eventually, the Scandinavian settlers in Britain adopted English, while Danish names for villages, forests, farms, and natural landmarks were in turn adopted by the English.

To this day, the name of a town ending in *-by* (which means farm or settlement) or *-thorp* (smaller settlement) shows the influence of the Danish Vikings. Whitby, Ingleby, Danby, and many other towns in eastern England still carry these suffixes. Other Danish names indicated features such as forests, streams, or prominent rocks. The English town of Caldbeck, for example, includes a form of the old Danish word *bekker,* which means "stream."

Scandinavian common nouns were also adopted by foreign languages. The words *birth, die, ugly, skin, kettle, smile,* and *mistake* are all words of Viking origin. The word *ransack,* from the Scandinavian word *rannsaka,* appears in modern English as well as Celtic and Norman French.

In Normandy, the Germanic language spoken by the followers of Rollo, who founded the realm in 911, was entirely different from the Latin-based language of the native French. The Danes of Normandy, like the Swedes of eastern Europe, had to adopt a new language in order to communicate with the people who surrounded them. In turn, the Normans gave their own names to certain villages and places in the Normandy countryside, where many of the inhabitants still carry physical traces— among them blond hair and blue eyes—of the thousand-year-old Viking colonization.

In areas where the Vikings formed a minority, their language was gradually replaced by that spoken by the majority. But in more sparsely populated areas, the Old Norse languages survived longer. The people of the Hebrides and the Isle of Man used Norse until the late Middle Ages. A Scandinavian dialect survived in the Shetland and Orkney Islands until the eighteenth century.

The Runes

Although the Viking language appears in place names and adapted words, little of it survives in written form. As far as archaeologists can tell, the Vikings did not use papyrus or parchment, the writing media of the Roman Empire and of medieval Europe, respectively. Instead, Viking writing exists only as marks, called runes, that were carved on standing stones and engraved on personal possessions.

The runes were first created in Germany in the time of the Roman Empire. Many scholars believe they were an adaptation of the Roman alphabet by the people of northern Europe. (For example, the runic letter for "B" resembles the modern Roman "B," using an upright line and two straight lines in a sideways "v" instead of half circles.) With trade contacts and migration, the runes spread among the different Germanic tribes of the European continent as well as the Scandinavians. There are runestones in Norway, Denmark, and in the Shetland and Orkney Islands, but for some reason, no runic inscriptions have survived in Iceland. Of all Scandinavian countries, Sweden has the most runic inscriptions; in Uppland (in east-central Sweden) alone more than one thousand carved runestones have been found.

The Vikings believed that the god Odin discovered the runes and their secret meanings by hanging himself for nine nights from the yew tree Yggdrasil. The scene is described in the *Havamal:*

> I know that I hung
> On the windswept tree
> For nine whole nights,
> Pierced by the spear
> And given to Odin—
> Myself given to myself
> On that tree
> Whose roots
> No one knows.
>
> They gave me not bread
> Nor drink from the horn;

A carved stone shows examples of runic writing. Since the Vikings left no paper records, runestones contain the only surviving examples of Norse writing.

Into the depths I peered,
I grasped the runes,
Screaming I grasped them,
And then fell back.[35]

Odin released magical powers from the runes, allowing these powers to be conjured and released by any man or woman initiated into their use.

The Futhark

The letters of the runic alphabet consist of straight and diagonal lines, which were easier to carve in a piece of wood or a slab of stone than were curved lines. The earliest runic alphabet is known as the futhark, after the names of the first six letters (f, u, th, a, r, and k), and is made up of twenty-four characters. At the beginning of the Viking age, a new sixteen-character alphabet, known as the later futhark,

came into use. But the later futhark was an incomplete way of writing Scandinavian languages; it had no letters for the consonants g, d, and p, nor for the vowels e and o. Rune writers had to substitute other letters to imitate these common sounds.

There were distinct styles of rune writing in different regions of the Viking world. Many rune writers had their own way of rendering words, letters, and phrases in their inscriptions. Some words were abbreviated; some letters were dropped; other letters were avoided for the sake of superstition. Many runic inscriptions were carved with a complicated code or secret magical formula in mind. Archaeologists still puzzle over the meanings of many of these runic inscriptions.

This mystery was deliberate: The runes were considered a magic code, to be understood only by a select few individuals. On gravestones, runes were carved in such a way that only the dead could see and benefit by them. Runes were also often inscribed on the unseen sides of weapons or implements, where, it was believed, they could best work the spells of protection and potency that gave swords an irresistible force or shields the power to deflect the sharpest of weapons.

In addition, the runes had a public use in commemorating important events or people. Runestones were set up to memorialize a dead chieftain or an important landowner who died in battle or while raiding in a distant land. The stones praised their subjects for their justness, ability as a warrior, generosity, or noble lineage. Other runestones were carved simply to record the presence of their creator. A Swedish Viking carved his name in runic letters into a balustrade in a cathedral in the Byzantine city of Constantinople (modern-day Istanbul,

Turkey). A partial runic inscription from the fourteenth century was found in Greenland, well north of the Arctic Circle at seventy-three degrees latitude, by an Inuit. The broken rune lay inside a stone cairn and said only, "Saturday before the minor Rogation Day [April 25], Erling Sighvatsson and Bjarni Thordarson and Eindridi Jonsson erected these cairns and. . . ." [36]

Late in the Viking age runestones began to carry Christian symbols and references to events and people in the Bible. The most famous Viking runestones are the Jelling stones, carved during the Jelling dynasty of Denmark. In the Jelling stones, Harold II Bluetooth proudly records his conquest of Norway and Denmark and his conversion of the Danes to Christianity. Meanwhile, in Norway

Jarlabanke's Runes

Sweden has more than three thousand surviving runic inscriptions, more than any other country. In his book *Vikings!*, historian Magnus Magnusson describes how one set of still-standing runes marks the conversion of a wealthy Swedish Viking from the old pagan religion to Christianity.

A land route called the Viking Road (*Vikingavegen*) was built through Uppland in the ninth century to supplement the communication system based on water and ice. This route was punctuated by memorial stones, especially at bridges where they were particularly useful as road markers in deep snow. This extension of the transport system grew apace with the internal structure of the state itself. . . .

We see it happening through the rune stones at one particular stretch of the Viking Road in the district of Taby, just outside

of Stockholm. Early in the eleventh century, responsibility for the upkeep of that stretch belonged to a powerful local landowner called Jarlabanke. He took his duties seriously and put up about twenty inscribed stones along the way. Two magnificent pairs of matching stones are still to be seen *in situ* [in their original site] at a new causeway he built—Jarlabankesbro—which was 115 meters long and seven meters wide: "Jarlabanke had these stones raised in memory of himself while he still lived. And he built this bridge for his soul. And alone he owned the whole of Taby. God help his soul!" Good works of this practical kind are evidence of the growing influence of the missionary church in Sweden; converts were encouraged to provide roads that would be serviceable in all weather to enable people to reach God's houses.

around the year 1000, Pope Gregory ordered Olaf I Trygvasson to adopt the Latin alphabet as a condition of bringing his country under the authority of the Catholic Church. Olaf complied, and soon afterward the magical and everyday use of the runes began to die out in Scandinavia.

Viking Poetry

The runes were a practical, useful item, but they were not used for storytelling or poetry. Instead, Viking poetry survives only in the lines of the skalds, the professional poets who sang and recited for Viking nobles and chieftains. Skaldic poetry recounted familiar legends of the gods and heroes of Norse mythology as well as the deeds of living and dead kings. To construct their works, the skalds used complex rhyming schemes and poetic devices known as kennings. A kenning is a compound word or phrase used as a metaphor. Some kennings were as simple as using the phrase "sea steed" for "ship," or "shield-biter" for "axe." Other kennings were complex and nearly impossible for the skald's listeners, and modern readers, to untangle: "the fjord elk's plains' fire," for example, meant "gold."[37]

Eventually the poems and stories passed down from one generation to the next were written down. Contact with European traders and missionaries brought the custom of recording such stories to Scandinavia. Professional scribes and scholars were hired by wealthy families to make these works perma-

A pair of the renowned Jelling stones. In runes and pictures, these stones relate the tale of Harold Bluetooth's conquest of Norway and Denmark and his conversion of the Danes to Christianity.

nent by recording them. To carry out their task, the scribes used quill feathers, ink made from the juice of berries, and sheets of thin vellum, made from the skin of calves or lambs. They adapted the Roman alphabet to the language of the Vikings, and the modern alphabets used to write the languages of Scandinavia were born.

The works of the skalds were written down in the Middle Ages in a collection known as the *Poetic Edda*, which included poems about the Viking gods and heroes. In the *Edda's* first poem, *Voluspa,* the poet gives a survey of the creation and eventual destruction of the world according to the beliefs of the Vikings. The next poem in the collection is the *Havamal,* or *Sayings of the High One.* The *Havamal* contains many short aphorisms that served to advise, guide, and warn its Viking readers and listeners. Skaldic poetry also was preserved in the long prose tales known as sagas.

The Sagas

The best-known sagas were written in Iceland in the twelfth and thirteenth centuries. By this time, and earlier than anywhere else in Europe, the common people of Iceland could read and write. They wrote down their laws, accounts of their families and ancestors, and religious works. One of the earliest books of Iceland was the *Landnamabok,* an account of the four hundred families who came from Norway, Ireland, and the Shetland Islands to first settle Iceland in the ninth century.

In their books and poems, the Icelanders also recounted the deeds and misdeeds of Harold Hardraade of Norway, the voyages of Eric the Red and his son Leif Eriksson in Greenland and Vinland, and the battles fought among Danes, Norwegians, and English before Britain was conquered by the

The Sayings of the High One

In his book *The Vikings,* historian Johannes Brondsted quotes these sayings from the *Havamal,* a poem including Viking aphorisms (short phrases of advice) that were said to come from the Norse god Odin himself.

"A coward thinks he will live forever if he avoids his enemies, but old age no man escapes even if he survives the spears."

"Never quarrel with a fool. A wise man will often refrain from fighting, whereas a fool will fight without cause or reason."

"A man should never move an inch from his weapons when in the fields, for he never knows when he will need his spear."

"A man who wishes to take another's life and goods must get up early. A wolf that lies in its lair never gets meat, nor a sleeping man victory."

"If you do not trust a man and yet want him to do you good, speak him fair; but think him false and give him treachery in return for his lies."

"A lame man can ride a horse; a man without hands can be a shepard; a deaf man can kill; it is better to be blind than to be burned on the funeral pyre. A dead man is of no use to anyone."

Normans in the year 1066. The author Snorri Sturluson, who lived from 1179 until 1241, wrote several Viking sagas based on poems that have since disappeared. Snorri regarded the poetry of the skalds as art as well as history. In one of his books, he explains,

Leif Eriksson lands in Vinland. The deeds of adventurers like Eriksson were often recounted in Icelandic sagas.

With King Harald there were skalds, and people still know their poems and poems about all the kings who have since then ruled in Norway. We have the greatest reliance on what is stated in those poems which were recited before the chieftains themselves or their sons. We regard as true everything which these verses relate about their expeditions and battles. It is the custom of skalds to praise him most highly before whom they are standing, yet no one would dare attribute to him deeds which he himself and all within hearing distance knew to be falsehood and fabrication, for that would be mockery and not praise.[38]

Snorri Sturluson is still revered as the national poet of Iceland. He was a wealthy landowner and a *godi* (chieftain) who glorified the Viking past with his long tales of brave deeds. His own life was turbulent and violent, as he spent much of his time intriguing against the king of Norway. Eventually, however, politics proved too dangerous even for him. On the night of September 23, 1241, a small army loyal to Snorri's rival, Gissur Thorvaldsson, arrived at his estate. One historian recounts that the invaders

went unchallenged through the sturdy stockade that Snorri had built around the farmhouse for just such an emergency, and then forced their way into the house. Snorri was asleep . . . but managed to get away. . . . Eventually they found him hiding in a cellar underneath the buildings. Five men went down into the cellar; and there, unarmed and defenceless, Iceland's most distinguished man of letters was struck down and killed.[39]

Viking Art

The Vikings left behind no written music, no books, and no paintings. But archaeologists have unearthed many examples of their skill as artists in picture stones, ornamented ships, decorated weapons and jewelry, and wood carvings. Although Viking artists are not known by name, they are recognized by their style and by their individual works. The artist who carved a certain work from a burial in Norway, for example, is called "the Academician." Another is known as "the Master of the Prow" for his work carving the heads on dragon ships. These artists were skilled craftsmen who worked in stone, silver, iron, and wood. One Viking historian, James Graham-Campbell, comments,

> The ornaments produced by jewellers provide our main source of evidence for the history of Viking art. The development of "fashionable" styles may be traced through the products of the gold- and silversmiths who worked to order for rich patrons, or sold their work to customers looking for means for ostentatious display of their wealth and rank.[40]

Viking artists may also have learned techniques from the lands their countrymen were raiding and plundering. In this way, the flowing, interlacing lines of illuminated Irish and Anglo-Saxon manuscripts, such as *The Book of Kells,* found their way into the decorative brooches and sword hilts used by the northern pagans.

A carving that decorates a Norse ship illustrates the intricate detail that characterizes Viking art.

Many Viking works depict wild or mythical animals: lions, dragons, snakes, and the purely imaginary creature known as the "gripping beast." The gripping beast could resemble a long, curving serpent, a bird, or a dragon. It often had huge staring eyes and claws that gripped anything nearby: the limbs of another imaginary beast, the curved sides of a brooch, or the edge of a harness. The gripping beast could be shaped and stretched to fill the spaces in a flat surface or a three-dimensional object. It was the most popular motif in all of Viking art, and it was used in many different styles and in different periods.

Viking Styles

Historians have identified and described several different Viking art styles, much as art historians have grouped modern works into styles such as Cubism, Impressionism, and Expressionism. The Borre style, one of the earliest strictly Viking art styles, was used during the years 850 through 950. Borre artists often used circles, squares, and a long double ribbon that spiraled about the surface and edges of brooches, pins, and drinking cups. In the Jellinge style, which was common in the tenth century, the Borre ribbon turned into a decorative S-shaped animal, like an elongated, abstract snake or dragon. In some pieces, several of these shapes are twisted together in an intricate pattern, as the lines of one beast crisscross the lines of another.

The Mammen style developed out of the Jellinge style and is named after a silver-inlaid axe head dated to about 970 that was found in Denmark. The lines of the Mammen style were thicker than in the earlier styles. The Mammen style was the first to borrow the designs of leaves and plants that were then popular in western Europe; it was also the first Viking style to include biblical scenes. The most famous Mammen sculpture is the Jelling stone of Denmark, which shows a crucifixion.

Picturing the Gripping Beast

In *A History of the Vikings,* historian Gwyn Jones describes the gripping beast that adorned many Viking artworks.

"We have no certain indication of where this exciting little creature came from. Some give him an ancestry in Carolingian lion-forms; others derive all his features from earlier Scandinavian work. . . . Lion, dog, cat, bear are among his suggested constituents. The head is large, the eyes goggling, the nose blobbed, the mouth small. The forehead is baldish, and the back of the head carries a pigtail or scalplock. The expression of the full face can be at once fierce and comic. The body varies in width but the waist is thin; the thighs can be plump and pear-shaped. His paws (one would prefer to say hands and feet) give him his name: they are for ever gripping the sides of his frame, a neighboring animal, some portion of himself, or sometimes all of these together. . . . Grotesque, varied, ferocious, filled with energy, and lending itself to sallies of virile wit and humour, the gripping beast seems to have fascinated Scandinavian artists of the ninth century, who with all their interest in animal motifs had never found one quite so intriguing as this."

Viking artists developed a new style known as Ringerike in the late tenth century. The Ringerike style was named after a group of decorated standing stones in Norway. Ringerike artists carved many such stones as well as pictures of the saints in the earliest Scandinavian churches. Long, thick tendrils sprout from the plant motifs; the many small and complex gripping beasts were transformed into a single, large beast that stands alone, its arms, legs, and tail ending in delicate spirals. In some Ringerike works, the great beast shares the space with a smaller serpent.

The Urnes style, which began in the mid–eleventh century, was the last purely Viking art style. Artists working in the Urnes style depicted lions, snakes, and dragons, linked with looping figure-eights that give an illusionary three-dimensional background. The Urnes style was used in many early Scandinavian churches. It was also adopted by metalsmiths and artists in Great Britain and Ireland.

As contact with Europe increased, the old Viking styles were left behind and Scandinavian architects and artists adopted the Romanesque style that prevailed in the rest of Europe. The complex, looping lines were dropped for a more solid and simple look, even while certain old animal motifs remained in medieval altar pieces, sculptures, and tapestries. Historian James Graham-Campbell explains:

> Although Viking art remained true to its traditions for three centuries, despite borrowings from other cultures, by the twelfth century the vitality had gone out of it. So there was no resistance to the impact of the new Romanesque art. Romanesque art, with its robust qualities and occasional grotesqueries, in fact had much that appealed to Scandinavian taste; while at the same time it is hardly surprising that el-

An example of the Urnes style carries the telltale figure-eights that connect the prominent images.

ements of the Urnes style occasionally found their way into the Romanesque of Scandinavia, Ireland and England.

Indeed in the remoter valleys and fjords of Scandinavia the motifs of Viking art lived on. A Norwegian wooden harness bow of the twelfth century or later is covered with a gripping-beast motif; the Borre ring-chain continued to turn up all over the place in Scandinavian folk art.[41]

Viking art, however, practically disappeared as the Viking era faded. The traces that remained were bound up in the continental European styles that came to dominate Scandinavian design.

Viking Religion

The Viking religion was polytheistic: It included many gods, some important, some minor, but each having a certain role to play in human affairs. Some gods were distant and powerful, while others were more familiar, more "human," making them playful, mischievous, or friendly. The gods of the Vikings belonged to the Germanic pantheon that had come north with the first migrants into Norway, Denmark, and Sweden. Some of them, such as Odin, remained identical with these gods while others, over the years that the Scandinavians lived apart in their more northerly regions, underwent transformations and took on new names.

The Creation of the World

The Vikings, like the Christians, believed that in the beginning the world was void, chaotic, and without form. They even had a word for this void: *Ginnungagap*. As Viking poets told it, the god Odin and his brothers arranged the earth, the sun, the moon, and the seasons. The home of the gods, Asgard, was built, as was Midgard, the realm of human beings, and Utgard, the edge of the world where the giants lived.

At the very center of creation stands Yggdrasil, or the world tree, also known as "Odin's horse." Odin, the most powerful of all Viking deities, hanged himself from Yggdrasil to gain knowledge of the runes. The gods assembled under this tree to dispute; the three

norns, or fates, also gathered there. The world tree was also the target of the destructive gods and forces that would eventually bring about the end of the world in a catastrophic event known as Ragnarok.

Odin

Odin is still the best known of all Viking gods—even people who know nothing about Odin still use his name for the day of the week known in the English language as Wednesday ("Odin's Day"). In many Viking depictions of Odin, a raven sits on his shoulder while he grapples with the wolf Fenris, who attacks Odin's leg, and who, at the end of the world, will eventually destroy the god. Johannes Brondsted describes Odin as

> a magnificent, dominating, demonic, and sadistic figure. He is consumed by his passion for wisdom; for its sake he sacrifices an eye, even hangs himself. Pitiless, capricious, heartless, he is the god of war and of the slain warriors. He owns the spear, Gungni, the self-renewing gold ring, Draupni, the fleet eight-footed horse, Sleipnir. He is guarded by his two wolves and is brought news from everywhere by his two ravens.[42]

Odin was a practitioner of *seid*, the shamanistic magic of the Vikings in which a sorcerer makes contact with the gods through chanting. Odin then gave this knowledge to a select group of humans. According to historians Prudence Jones and Nigel Pennick, this magic manifested itself as a belief in clairvoyance in pagan Scandinavia:

> It is clear from the sagas and the Icelandic Settlement Book that it was common for people to have second sight or to work magic to see into the future. Even the Christian Queen Dowager Aud of Dublin, a late settler in Iceland, knew when she was going to die. She held a feast, which she declared would be her funeral feast, correctly predicting her death three days later.[43]

An image of Odin astride his eight-legged steed. The ravens that bring him the news of the world circle about him.

The Aesir and the Vanir

The Vikings arranged their gods into two rival groups: the Aesir and the Vanir. The Aesir are the gods who preside over magic, over war, and over wisdom. The Vanir gods included Njord, the god of winds, weather, and sailors; Freya, a goddess of fertility; and Frey, the most important of the Vanir among the Vikings. Frey was a god of farming, who could assist in bringing good crops, raising healthy livestock herds, and the fertility of a young married couple. In representations of Frey, he often wears a long beard and a pointed cap.

The Vanir were all that remained in Viking times of an even more ancient fertility cult that was dying out in Scandinavia. In many myths, the Aesir struggle and fight with the Vanir, just as among the Vikings a new religion of the Aesir was replacing the old (and would in turn be replaced by Christianity).

Thor and Loki

Thor was the largest and strongest of the gods. He was the god who strived in battle against the giants. He wore a red beard and drove a chariot pulled by goats (the rumble of the chariot was thought to be responsible for the noise of thunder). Thor used a war hammer named Mjollnir in his fight against the Vanir. As protective talismans, both Viking men and women commonly wore small, T-shaped amulets that were known as Thor's hammers.

Loki was an entirely different sort of god. He was constantly playing mean tricks on the other gods of the Aesir, out of sheer jealousy. "Fickle and false, clever and cunning, the trickster god Loki was 'the father of lies,'"[44] reports historian K. R. G. Pendlesohn, who also claims that Loki originated in the destructive

Thor, the strongest of the gods, brandishes his hammer as he is pulled through the heavens in his chariot.

and unpredictable forest fires that sometimes ravaged the northern forests. Loki's cleverness, however, often landed him in serious trouble. He once made a bet with a dwarf, gambling his own head. After losing the wager, he informed the dwarf that he had not made any mention of his neck. For this, the dwarf sewed Loki's lips together, a trait that can be seen on some representations of the god.

A Cast of Gods and Giants

There were many more characters in the religion of the Vikings. The Fylgjur or Valkyries were women who were present in the skies during a battle, attending to human and divine warriors. They selected the heroes who were to die in battle and accompanied them to the great hall of Valhalla, the final feasting place of Viking heroes. These heroes were brought to the hall on Odin's eight-legged horse, Sleipnir, and spent their evenings in feasting, roasting a pig named Sarimner that

returned to life the next day only to be slaughtered and roasted again. By day, the warriors of Valhalla donned armor and weapons to fight on a nearby field, where they happily spent their time cutting, chopping, and spearing each other only to return to the feasting hall to celebrate again.

The norns, sometimes confused with Valkyries, are the three goddesses, or fates, who ride in the sky over battlefields, sometimes coming down to earth to interfere in the combat or to turn the luck of a warrior they favored. The Vikings gave the greatest respect to the norns because they believed that dying in battle and going to Valhalla was a much better fate than dying peacefully in their beds, which would bring them to a cold, foggy, boring place called Niflheim.

Besides fighting among themselves, the gods of Asgard were often pitted against the inhabitants of Utgard. The Jotun, a hostile race of giants, opposed the Aesir and the Vanir and their system and typically sought to destroy it. But the Jotun were not always depicted as foes; the gods allied with, and even married, giants. Gro Steinsland describes this paradox:

> [The giants represent] primeval powers who want to destroy the order of the gods. But the gods were also dependent on the giants: in the language of myth it is said that the giants possess objects and wisdom which the gods need. . . . Gods and giants enter alliances, for example marriage: in a sacred wedding of a deity and a giantess lies the origin of a new dynasty of kings or earls. Gods and giants are thus simultaneously opposites and allies in a dynamic process, the evolution of the world.[45]

Living with the Gods

In the Viking world, the gods, goddesses, and spirits lived in close proximity to human beings. This pagan array of supernatural beings was believed to be ever-present, watching

---

The Hammer of Thor

One of the most common articles found in Viking graves and archaeological sites is the Mjollnir, or "the Hammer of Thor." This small, T-shaped pendant was worn as a protective amulet by men and women throughout Scandinavia (other Viking amulets were made of animal teeth or bear claws). They have been found in graves throughout northern Europe as well as the British Isles, Russia, and Iceland. Some of Thor's hammers are made of plain, undecorated silver; others are iron, bronze, or amber; a few are elaborately crafted gold or silver works of master jewelers.

Thor was one of the most powerful and important Viking gods. He protected peasants and their farms and sided with ordinary people in their struggles against bad luck and the elements. He was a fertility god whose name was invoked at the spring planting and at Viking weddings. Around the late-night fire, the Vikings told stories of Thor riding in a chariot pulled by goats and battling enemy gods and giants armed with Mjollnir, his mighty hammer. Whenever thunder and lightning struck the earth, it was believed that Thor was striving somewhere in Asgard, the home of the gods.

Despite his power and his popularity, Thor lost his final battle, in which all the gods of the Aesir and the Vanir were replaced by the Christian god of the Bible. Many people of the late Viking age wore Thor's hammers as a symbol of their resistance to conversion and to the cross, the symbol of the new faith. Beginning in the early eleventh century, however, Thor and Mjollnir became folk memories of a dead religion, and Thor's hammers disappeared from the everyday clothing worn by the people of Scandinavia.

A smith's mold for casting both Thor's hammers and Christian crosses.

---

over the activities of the world from their sacred spots in the mountains, rocks, and trees among which humans moved. The gods had their all-too-human characteristics: Some were violent and dangerous, others were jealous, still others were simply mischievous. Occasionally a god would fall out of use, fade away, and be forgotten, to be replaced by a new and stronger god. Ull, for example, was an old god of hunting who was once worshipped in parts of Norway and Sweden. By Viking times, however, Ull was on the way out; his myths were forgotten and his image was ignored by Viking artists.

The Vikings named their gods, traded familiar stories about them, and created representations of them in jewelry and in stone and wood carvings. In this form, a favorite god accompanied a Viking man or woman as he or she went about the day's work. When in need, a Viking farmer or warrior could also call on his god to lend assistance or guidance at the start of the planting season or during a battle.

Norsemen carved depictions of their gods on both significant and common items. Here, a representation has been affixed to a bucket handle.

Places of worship were set up outdoors, usually at a certain old tree or grove or near a rock or riverside. A watchful image of the god, carved in wood or stone, might be present nearby. Later, temples of wood or stone were raised on these sacred spots. During a pagan ceremony, it was common for a priest or chieftain to direct the sacrifice of a favorite animal: a horse, ox, sheep, or cow. The animal's blood was allowed to pour into a sacred bowl and then might be sprinkled about the temple and on the heads of all those present. The flesh of the animals was cooked and eaten. Humans were also sacrificed, usually by hanging from a certain sacred tree in imitation of the god Odin.

Celebrations

In celebration of a harvest or an important event, or to honor a favored god, the Vikings always held a feast. The feast might be arranged by a single family or by an entire clan. Cities such as Hedeby and Birka held big celebrations of their own. A Moor from Spain, Ibn al-Tartushi, witnessed one such celebration at Hedeby in about 950. "A feast is held to honor their deity," al-Tartushi reported, "Any man who slaughters a sacrificial animal—whether it is an ox, ram, goat, or pig—fastens it up on poles outside his house to show that he has made his sacrifice."[46]

The host prepared a table piled high with roasted meats and stews; if he was wealthy enough, he might flavor the dishes with rare and expensive spices brought from the Middle East. There were breads, vegetables, and nuts spread about, as well as ale and mead, and in wealthy households, wine. The halls of kings or chieftains might have wine goblets as well as plates of finely worked silver. Drinking horns might be used to pass the ale or mead from one guest to another; since the horns could not be put down until emptied, the feast quickly grew merry.

With the king or head of the household sitting at the place of honor at the center of the table, the company traded stories. A saga of the deeds of gods or heroes, appropriate to the occasion, would be recited. Music would also be on hand; the Vikings are known to have made small wooden flutes carved out of animal bones. Ibn al-Tartushi, however, was not impressed with Viking singing: "I have never heard such horrible singing," he complained after his visit to Hedeby. "It is like a growl coming out of their throats, like the barking of dogs only still more brutish."[47]

The most important religious celebrations were known as *blot*. As historian Gro Steinsland writes,

> To *blota* means to strengthen, and it was the gods who had to be given strength for their tasks by means of people's cult activities, of which sacrifice was the most important. Horses or pigs were slaughtered, people gathered around the sacred rites and the steaming cooking pots. The blood of sacrificed animals was especially sacred. The sacred drink, mead, was consecrated to the gods and they were toasted in it. The departed ancestors were also remembered with toasts. . . . In their sacred drunkenness people would have felt a strengthening of their own fellowship, as well as their fellowship with the higher powers. There was feasting in hall, and scalds recited myths and composed verses about the deeds of gods and heroes.[48]

The Celebration of Yule

These celebrations took place during the changing of seasons, when the pagan gods were brought down to the earth to bring prosperity to the home and the village. At the winter solstice, all labor ceased for twelve days while the people waited for sun and daylight to return to the sky. The winter solstice feast was called Jul; it was dedicated to Frey and marked the end of seasonal labor in the fields. This festival survives as the twelve-day celebration of Christmas—Yule—in modern Scandinavia. It was a celebration of family, clan, and of deceased relatives, who returned from their graves to join their family again. Eric Oxenstierna describes the scene:

> A magnificent Yule table was set up for deceased relatives. A steam bath was readied for them, beds were freshly made, and the peasants slept on straw pallets on the floor so that those "from outside" could use the best rooms, take delight in all the luxuries, warm and satiate themselves. For they came out of the mounds, naturally, covered with earth or, if they had died at sea, wet and dripping. They sat with the living evening after evening, for as long as the feast lasted. We hear most often of exceptional cases, when the departed sat quietly presaging misfortune, dried their clothes by the fire and went back to their graves without having said a word.[49]

One of the most solemn celebrations in all of Scandinavia was the spring feast and sacrifice held at Uppsala, Sweden. The sacrifice was held once every nine years at the spring equinox. Nine male animals of various species were sacrificed and hung from trees in a sacred grove near the Uppsala temple, the most famous pagan temple of the Viking age. Those who had converted to the Christian faith could excuse themselves from the pagan ceremony by a payment of money.

Funeral Customs

Death was another occasion for the Vikings to encounter their gods and practice their faith, and the Vikings knew death well. Disease, hunger, accidents, and fighting took many lives; few Vikings lived long enough to experience a peaceful old age. (In some isolated, poor communities, such as the lonely outposts on Greenland, men and women commonly died before reaching the age of forty.) Those who left on long and perilous voyages knew there was a good chance they would never see their home again; capture and enslavement by foreigners, or death in battle, were very possible. The Vikings prepared themselves for death, knowing that life was a single stop on a long journey that simply changed directions at the time of their passing.

Among the Vikings, there was no single way to bury, equip, or memorialize the dead. They might be cremated on a pyre, laid to rest in their ships, or simply placed, fully clothed, in the ground. But the Vikings always took care to equip their dead for the voyages of the afterlife. Men were buried with their weapons, favorite tools, and battle armor, if they owned any. Small balance scales show that a grave holds a merchant; tools for working iron reveal the grave of a smith. Often these articles were damaged in some way (swords were bent double, for example), so that they would be of

A Funeral Among the Vikings

In his book *AD 1000*, historian Richard Erdoes relates the strange experience of the Arab traveler Ibn Fadlan, who, in his story of his travels among the Rus, left the world's only firsthand account of a Viking funeral.

"They had drawn the deceased lord's biggest ship on shore and put on board his long bench, covering it with Greek brocade. Then appeared an old hag whom they called 'the Angel of Death.' It is she who will kill the girl who agreed to die with her master, and truly she did not look like an angel but like the devil. They put into the ship much intoxicating drink and his harp, fruit, basil, meat, and onions. They took his favorite dog, cut him in two, and threw the parts into the ship. They also killed horses and two oxen, cut them into pieces and threw these also into the ship.

They had made a thing looking like a gate with protruding eaves. . . . Then they led [the girl] to the ship. She took off her two armlets, giving them to the death-angel who was about to murder her. She took off her ankle rings and gave them to the two maidservants of the old hag. Then came the men with shields and stick handing her a cup of numbing drink. She took it, sang, and emptied it, taking leave of life. They gave her another, larger bowl to drink. She took it, intoning a lengthy song. The old she-devil told her to hurry up and go where her master was lying dead, but the girl hesitated. Quick as lightning, the old hag grabbed the girl by the hair, dragging her to the corpse. At once, all the men began to beat their shields with the stick, making a loud noise so that one should not hear the screams of the girl which might discourage others to follow her example.

The old woman quickly put a rope around the girl's neck, handing the ends to two men who began pulling with all their might. At the same time the death-angel plunged her broad-bladed knife between the girl's ribs. And so she died."

A dead Viking warrior is set adrift in a ship. His vessel is stocked with all the goods that were thought to be of use in the afterlife.

better use in the mysterious afterworld. Their favorite horse or a slave might also be killed to accompany them. Women were commonly buried with jewelry and household goods. In some parts of Scandinavia, tradition had the family of the dead burn the body on a pyre, along with some private possessions, then bury the ashes under a mound.

Burial Mounds

For Viking kings and chieftains, immense mounds were raised. Several mounds might be reserved for a powerful chieftain, who could then travel from one mound to the next, visiting his far-flung realm as he pleased. These empty mounds can prove frustrating for modern archaeologists. At Raknehaugen,

Norway, the hard work of excavating a burial mound fifty feet high and more than three hundred feet in diameter was begun in 1939, but historian Eric Oxenstierna relates that

> nothing was found but three stout wooden layers, consisting of uprights, as in a charcoal kiln, which in this case never burned but, in the course of centuries, rotted. To the historian of antiquity, the wooden structure looks like a funeral pyre and might well be a royal cenotaph [empty tomb] of Viking days, older even than the ship graves of the Vestfold kings. Of course the scholar's heart is left a bit hollow, too, with such meager findings after such hard work: 78,840 cubic yards of earth were moved . . . for a man who wasn't even buried in his mound![50]

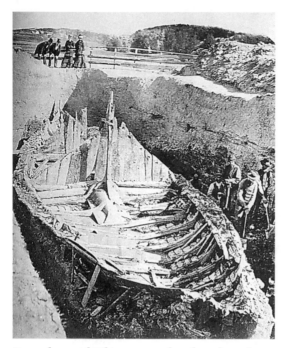

Some deceased Vikings were placed on their ships and then the entire craft was buried in the ground. Here, an excavation of the Gokstad ship shows the gables of the burial chamber at the rear.

In many parts of the Viking world, burial or cremation in a ship was the traditional method for seeing a leader off on his final voyage. The ship was fully equipped with protective tents or chambers; chests, clothing, furniture, carts and sleighs, draft animals such as oxen and horses, even household pets might also be placed aboard. The most spectacular archaeological finds were the ship burials at Oseberg and Gokstad in the Oslo fjord region of southern Norway. In 1880 archaeologists uncovered the Gokstad ship, seventy-six feet long and seventeen feet at its widest point. Historian Robert Wernick describes its discovery:

> In the early new year of 1880, some country people on the Gokstad farm in Sandar, Norway, started poking into a large bar-

row of earth that since time out of mind had been known as the King's Mound. It stood on a flat, treeless plain and was understood to be the tomb of a great Viking king. No one had dared disturb the mound before, but now curiosity got the better of superstition.

> News of the venture spread to Oslo, where the government wisely decided not to let the excavation go unsupervised. The project was placed under the direction of an eminent Norwegian antiquarian, N. Nicolaysen—and not a moment too soon. Two days after Nicolaysen arrived on the scene, the prow of a huge wooden ship was unearthed. . . . The enormous oaken craft was the first complete Viking ship ever uncovered.[51]

The ship was preserved in blue clay; on its deck was a burial chamber that contained the skeleton of a man who had died around A.D. 900. Accompanying the man on his final journey were smaller boats, beds, household utensils such as buckets and cups, as well as horses, dogs, and a pet peacock. (In 1893 a replica of the Gokstad ship was built. The boat was sailed from Sweden to Newfoundland in twenty-eight days.)

Not far from Gokstad another ship was discovered in 1904. The ship was beautifully carved and contained the remains of two women. Inside the burial chamber were several beds and quilts, carts, chests, sleds, utensils, a dozen horses, household pets, food, and spices. The Oseberg ship was a ceremonial craft that some historians believe held the remains of Queen Asa, the wife of Gudrod the Magnificent. Two female skeletons were found within the ship, one much older and more frail, probably a slave or servant of the other.

Later, as Scandinavia converted to Christianity, cemeteries were moved to the hallowed ground adjoining the town church. The dead were buried in a simple burial shroud; their bodies were laid down in an east-west direction according to Christian tradition. The practice of burying objects or animals with them ceased.

The End of the World

The end of the world, according to the Vikings, would take place during a spectacular event known as Ragnarok. According to the stories told around the hearths and campfires of the north, strange, frightening portents would herald the coming of Ragnarok. Garm, a gigantic hound, begins to howl, while the serpent of Midgard rains venom down from the sky.

The sound of the god Heimdall blowing his trumpet finally announced the start of Ragnarok. Odin calls all the gods and heroes from Valhalla to fight a last final battle against the forces of evil. The battle takes place on an immense field called Vigrid and pits the Aesir against the Vanir. The two sides begin to slaughter each other. Loki and Heimdall fight to the death, Odin is killed by the wolf Fenris, and Thor is poisoned by the Midgard serpent. At the end, all the gods and the heroes who have joined them lie dead. "The earth is afire," according to one account. "Flames spurt from

cracks in a charred earth. The rivers boil. The world is swallowed up by foaming waters. A black sun turns to ice. Nothing is left. All is finished." [52]

The myth of the dreaded Ragnarok gave the Vikings a grim outlook on life. There was no redemption waiting at the end of the world, as there may be for Christians, so the Vikings did not see the necessity of redeeming themselves for the chance at reaching paradise. Instead, they most admired the ability of an individual to struggle against, and eventually come to terms with, his fate, no matter how dire and hopeless it may be.

The Conversion of the Vikings

The Vikings first met Christian believers during their trading voyages across the North Sea to Europe and Britain. To more easily deal with these Christians, who saw the pagan gods as backwards and barbarian, Viking merchants made a show of accepting some simple Christian rites. Some allowed themselves to be baptized; others were "prime signed," meaning they had the gesture of the cross made before them by a Christian priest or bishop.

But these merchants, and the Viking raiders who followed them, were not true converts. For them, accepting Christianity was a convenient way to do business—or a trick to conquer a city. According to one story, a Viking raiding party under a leader named Hasteinn once planned to attack the greatest Christian city of all, Rome. As historian Holger Arbman writes,

> The defenses of their objective proved too strong and they had to resort to cunning in order to gain entrance; they pretended that their leader had died and that they desired for him Christian burial. Once the bier was safely inside the town the "dead" Hasteinn leapt from it and ran the bishop through.[53]

The Vikings easily took the city but soon found, to their embarrassment, that they had not conquered Rome but instead the small port town of Luna.

A New Faith Arrives

Beginning in the ninth century, missionaries from Europe arrived to convert the Vikings to Christianity. The first church at Birka in Sweden was built by a missionary named Ansgar in the 830s. Over the next few centuries, a few Swedish kings accepted Christianity, and runestones sometimes carried images and expressions of the new faith.

Eventually, Scandinavian kings such as Harold II Bluetooth of Denmark and Olaf I Trygvasson of Norway converted their people by force or decree to Christianity. Olaf was raised in Russia as an exile from his own country. He had raided coasts from the Baltic Sea to the northern tip of Britain and was convinced by a fortune-teller to accept Christianity. He then mounted a violent campaign against the pagan believers of his homeland, sailing back to Norway with an invading force. Olaf plundered every pagan temple he could find and destroyed the wooden idols of the pagan gods. Those who refused to convert to Christianity were killed.

In Iceland conversion was carried out much more peacefully. Instead of fighting over the new religion, the Icelanders debated what to do at their annual assembly at Thingvellir. In the year 1000, one speaker at the assembly, Thorgeirr Ljosvetningagodi, proposed that the people of Iceland must adopt a single faith, whatever it may be. After his listeners agreed, he continued by proposing that "all people in

Iceland were to be baptized and believe in one God. . . . People should be permitted to hold pagan sacrificial feasts in secret if they wished to, but under penalty of the lesser outlawry if this were discovered."[54] Thus, the two beliefs coexisted for some time before paganism died out entirely in Iceland.

Throughout Scandinavia Christian authorities appropriated and transformed traditional Norse pagan festivals. One was the Jul festival, which was transformed into the celebration of Christ's birth at Christmastime. To determine the date of Christ's actual birth,

Hasteinn awakes from his feigned death in order to destroy what he thinks is Rome, the capital of Christianity. Such attempts to topple the Christian faith were ineffectual; widespread conversion to Christianity ended the Viking era.

the Christian Church marked nine months from the date of the Annunciation. This date, by coincidence, fell right around the pagan winter solstice festival.

The people of Scandinavia also raised new Christian churches directly over the old pagan temples. At the cathedral in Uppsala in Sweden, postholes were found that archaeologists believe belong to a former pagan temple. Cemeteries were placed in consecrated ground close to the church, away from the families and clans that had once presided over the burial of their own dead. Christian bishops now laid down the rites to mark baptism, to celebrate marriages, and to preside at funerals. In Scandinavia only the Lapps of the far north remained pagan until the seventeenth and eighteenth centuries; like the Vikings, they too were converted by missionaries from the south.

The End of the Viking Era

The Viking era began with violent raiding by a northern, pagan society. The end of that same era is marked by the Christianization of the Scandinavians. In Denmark King Harold Bluetooth converted his nation in the 960s. Sweden was the last Scandinavian country to adopt Christianity, at the end of the eleventh century. The conversion took several centuries, and many northerners fiercely resisted it. Others reluctantly took up the new faith but continued to participate in the traditional feasts and sacrifices that honored their former gods. One Christian noted in the twelfth century that

> Swedes . . . seem certainly, as long as everything goes well for them, to hold in name the Christian faith in honor. But when the storms of misfortune come over them, if the earth denies them her crops

or heaven her rain, storms rage, or fire destroys, then they condemn Christianity . . . through pursuit of believing Christians whom they seek to drive from the country.[55]

As in the rest of Europe, old temples dedicated to the pagan gods were torn down and replaced by Christian churches. Scandinavian artists began depicting biblical scenes on tapestries, on stone carvings, and on woodwork. Christianity brought important changes to the traditions of inheritance and marriage and to the law. A minimum age for marriage was set down by religious authorities, polygamy was prohibited, and baptism in the Christian Church became a requirement for inheritance. The practice of cremation ended; the Scandinavians now buried their dead in simple graves, without grave goods, and dressed the dead without jewelry, weapons, or finery of any sort.

Bishops were established in the largest towns, and the kings of Scandinavia forged alliances with them to extend their control over rival nobles and the common people. Obedience to the church went hand-in-hand with obedience and service to the state. The personal faith of the pagan Vikings, each of whom had a personal god to call on in times of need or danger, was changed into a commonly held faith in a single god. The myths of the gods, told and retold over the family's hearth, changed into biblical stories and parables recited by church leaders in a common meeting ground, the church. Idols and amulets shaped in the images of Frey, Thor, and Odin were replaced by crucifixes and illustrations of the life of Christ.

The Viking era survived as a proud memory throughout Scandinavia. Today, the remains of the Vikings—their homes, burial mounds, ships, towns, and fortresses—are carefully marked and preserved historic sites. In Norway an entire museum is dedicated to the remains of the Oseberg ship and its contents; in Iceland ancient turf homes have been carefully reconstructed and Thingvellir, the site of Iceland's Althing, has become a national shrine. Throughout Europe museums exhibit Viking art as well as everyday household objects dug up from townsites, farms, and graves. Such sites and exhibits now remind visitors that the Viking society, which still holds many mysteries, ran much deeper than the simple image of pagan raiders who spent three centuries frightening the people of Europe.

Notes

Introduction: The Vikings: Legend and Reality

1. Eric Oxenstierna, *The Norsemen.* New York: New York Graphic Society, 1965, p. 14.
2. P. H. Sawyer, *The Age of the Vikings.* London: Camelot Press, 1962, p. 10.

Chapter 1: The Viking Encounter

3. Dorothy Whitelock, ed., *The Anglo-Saxon Chronicle.* New Brunswick, NJ: Rutgers University Press, 1961, p. 35.
4. Quoted in Holger Arbman, *The Vikings,* trans. and ed. Alan Binns. New York: Praeger, 1961, p. 50.
5. Whitelock, *The Anglo-Saxon Chronicle,* p. 36.
6. Quoted in Arbman, *The Vikings,* p. 68.
7. Arbman, *The Vikings,* pp. 68–69.
8. Quoted in Oxenstierna, *The Norsemen,* p. 16.
9. Quoted in Arbman, *The Vikings,* p. 79.
10. Peter Brent, *The Viking Saga.* New York: G. P. Putnam's Sons, 1975, p. 236.
11. Quoted in Arbman, *The Vikings,* p. 94.
12. Quoted in the Editors of Time-Life Books, *Vikings: Raiders from the North.* Alexandria, VA: Time-Life Books, 1993, p. 73.
13. H. G. Wells, *The Outline of History, Being a Plain History of Life and Mankind.* Garden City, NY: Garden City, 1931, p. 646.

Chapter 2: Viking Ships, Raiding, and Warfare

14. James Graham-Campbell, *The Viking World.* New York: Ticknor & Fields, 1980, p. 25.

15. Snorri Sturluson, *King Harald's Saga,* trans. Magnus Magnusson and Hermann Pálsson. New York: Penguin Books, 1966, pp. 107–108.
16. Sawyer, *The Age of the Vikings,* pp. 196–97.
17. Editors of Time-Life Books, *Vikings,* p. 104.
18. Robert Wernick, *The Vikings.* Alexandria, VA: Time-Life Books, 1979, p. 72.
19. Sturluson, *King Harald's Saga,* p. 123.
20. Wernick, *The Vikings,* p. 67.

Chapter 3: Viking Society

21. Johannes Brondsted, *The Vikings.* Baltimore: Penguin Books, 1965, p. 219.
22. Quoted in Brondsted, *The Vikings,* p. 224.
23. Quoted in Else Roesdahl and David M. Wilson, eds., *From Viking to Crusader: The Scandinavians and Europe, 800–1200.* New York: Rizzoli International, 1992, p. 126.
24. Quoted in Richard Erdoes, *AD 1000: Living on the Brink of Apocalypse.* San Francisco: Harper & Row, 1988, p. 151.
25. Quoted in Roesdahl and Wilson, *From Viking to Crusader,* p. 125.
26. Wernick, *The Vikings,* pp. 24, 133.

Chapter 4: Everyday Life Among the Vikings

27. Gwyn Jones, *A History of the Vikings.* Oxford, Great Britain: Oxford University Press, 1968, p. 167.
28. Magnus Magnusson, *Vikings!* New York: E. P. Dutton, 1980, p. 135.
29. Quoted in Graham-Campbell, *The Viking World,* p. 126.

30. Quoted in Oxenstierna, *The Norsemen,* p. 220.

Chapter 5: Farmers, Builders, and Traders

31. Quoted in Graham-Campbell, *The Viking World,* p. 12.
32. Quoted in Roesdahl and Wilson, *From Viking to Crusader,* p. 196.
33. Graham-Campbell, *The Viking World,* p. 128.
34. Oxenstierna, *The Norsemen,* p. 233.

Chapter 6: Viking Language, Art, and Poetry

35. Quoted in Magnusson, *Vikings!* p. 12.
36. Editors of Time-Life Books, *Vikings,* p. 158.
37. Sawyer, *The Age of the Vikings,* p. 38.
38. Quoted in Peter Hallberg, *The Icelandic Saga.* Lincoln: University of Nebraska Press, 1962, p. 40.
39. Sturluson, *King Harald's Saga,* p. 20.
40. Graham-Campbell, *The Viking World,* p. 140.
41. Graham-Campbell, *The Viking World,* pp. 152–53.

Chapter 7: Viking Religion

42. Brondsted, *The Vikings,* p. 274.
43. Prudence Jones and Nigel Pennick, *A History of Pagan Europe.* London: Routledge, 1995, pp. 149–50.
44. K. R. G. Pendlesohn, *The Vikings.* New York: Windward Books, 1980, p. 83.
45. Quoted in Roesdahl and Wilson, *From Viking to Crusader,* p. 144.
46. Quoted in the Editors of Time-Life Books, *Vikings,* p. 27.
47. Quoted in the Editors of Time-Life Books, *Vikings,* p. 28.
48. Quoted in Roesdahl and Wilson, *From Viking to Crusader,* p. 148.
49. Oxenstierna, *The Norsemen,* p. 217.
50. Oxenstierna, *The Norsemen,* p. 229.
51. Wernick, *The Vikings,* p. 36.
52. Erdoes, *AD 1000,* p. 138.

Epilogue: The Conversion of the Vikings

53. Arbman, *The Vikings,* p. 86.
54. Quoted in Hallberg, *The Icelandic Saga,* p. 13.
55. Quoted in Jones and Pennick, *A History of Pagan Europe,* p. 135.

Chronology of Events

ca. 700
Viking shipbuilders develop a large sail, tall masts, and heavy keels, allowing the Viking sailors to make long ocean voyages.

793
A Viking raiding party attacks the island monastery of Lindisfarne in Britain.

825
The people of Hedeby begin minting the first coins in Scandinavia.

829
The missionary Ansgar arrives in Birka, Sweden.

834
The Vikings begin raiding the Frankish trading center of Dorestad.

840
Norwegian Vikings found the trading center of Dublin, Ireland.

844
Vikings make first expedition to Moorish Spain.

860
Swedish Vikings make their first attacks on Byzantium.

870
Norwegian Vikings begin to settle Iceland.

900
The oldest known Scandinavian crucifix is made at the town of Hedeby.

911
The Danish leader Rollo is ceded Normandy by treaty with the king of the Franks.

930
The people of Iceland begin meeting in a general assembly, the Althing.

965
King Harold Bluetooth converts the people of Denmark to Christianity.

986
The first Viking settlement is built on Greenland.

1000
The people of Iceland agree to adopt Christianity after a debate at the annual assembly.

1066
A Norwegian army is defeated by the English at Stamford Bridge; a Norman army under William the Conqueror invades England.

14th century
Unable to grow food or trade with distant Europe, the old Viking colonies of Greenland die out.

For Further Reading

Michael Crichton, *Eaters of the Dead: The Manuscript of Ibn Fadlan, Relating His Experiences with the Northmen in* A.D. *922.* New York: Ballantine, 1976. A book that combines the diary of the Arab traveler Ibn Fadlan, who traveled among the Swedish Vikings (Rus) in the tenth century, and a fictionalized account of supernatural and terrifying happenings among the Rus.

Editors of Time-Life, *Vikings: Raiders from the North.* Alexandria, VA: Time-Life Books, 1993. A lightly written account of Viking history and society, richly illustrated with color images of artifacts, archaeological sites, maps, and modern-day memorials to the Viking legacy.

Peter Hicks, *Technology in the Time of the Vikings.* Austin, TX: Raintree Steck-Vaughn, 1998. Examines many of the technological innovations that the Vikings incorporated into their daily lives in such areas as weaponry and armor, transportation, and jewelry-making.

Andrea Hopkins, *Harald the Ruthless: The Saga of the Last Viking Warrior.* New York: Henry Holt, 1996. Retells the saga, as written by Snorri Sturluson, of the bloody conquests of a ruthless Norwegian leader whose death came during the campaign for England in 1066.

John James, *How We Know About the Vikings.* New York: P. Bedrick, 1997. An illustrated survey of the history, customs, religion, politics, and everyday life of the Vikings.

Susan M. Margeson, *Vikings.* New York: Alfred A. Knopf, 1994. An account of Viking history, culture, and society illustrated with hundreds of photographs that reenact daily life among the Vikings.

Charman Simon, *Leif Eriksson and the Vikings.* Chicago: Childrens Press, 1991. Relates the adventures of the Norse explorer who left Greenland to sail west and found a colony in North America.

Snorri Sturluson, *King Harald's Saga.* Trans. Magnus Magnusson and Hermann Pálsson. New York: Penguin Books, 1966. The story of Harold Hardraade's life and campaigns, taken from Snorri Sturluson's *Heimskringla*.

Works Consulted

Holger Arbman, *The Vikings*. Trans. and ed. Alan Binns. New York: Praegar, 1961. A thorough and very opinionated survey of Viking archaeology, relating in clear language the physical evidence for what we know about Viking history and society.

Peter Brent, *The Viking Saga*. New York: G. P. Putnam's Sons, 1975. A scholar's view of the sagas of Scandinavia, from the earliest Viking-era poetry to the medieval prose poems. A full explanation of symbolism, style, and the historical background of saga writing.

Johannes Brondsted, *The Vikings*. Baltimore: Penguin Books, 1965. A book that goes beyond the surface fascination of the Viking age to explore economic and cultural links with Britain and the rest of Europe, the underlying motives for Viking raiding and exploration, and the gradual integration of Scandinavia with the rest of Europe. Also includes an excellent survey of Viking religion and deities and an account of the Viking conversion.

Ewan Butler, *The Horizon Concise History of Scandinavia*. New York: American Heritage, 1973. A general survey of Scandinavian history that provides an excellent introduction to the Viking age and its leading personalities.

Paul du Chailu, *The Viking Age*. New York: Scribner's Sons, 1889. A poetic, romantic interpretation of Viking history and religion.

Richard Erdoes, AD 1000: *Living on the Brink of Apocalypse*. San Francisco: Harper & Row, 1988. A gripping account of events in the years just before the millennium year of A.D. 1000, when Christianity was spreading north and gradually overtaking Europe's last pagan societies. The author vividly describes the violent world of the Vikings, northern Germans, and Slavs.

Bruce Gelsinger, ed., *Dictionary of the Middle Ages*. New York: Scribner, 1982. A twelve-volume encyclopedia of people, places, and events of the Middle Ages, from the fall of the western Roman Empire to the early Renaissance. Hundreds of experts and scholars contributed the meticulously researched entries, most of which have bibliographies as well as cross-references to other entries in the set.

James Graham-Campbell, *The Viking World*. New York: Ticknor & Fields, 1980. A series of short essays on different aspects of the Viking world. Includes a thorough explanation of the different Viking art styles as well as descriptions of techniques and motifs used by Viking artisans.

James Graham-Campbell and Dafydd Kidd. *The Vikings*. New York: William Morrow, 1980. A description of Viking culture and daily life, using maps, diagrams, and highly detailed color photographs to sketch a general survey.

Peter Hallberg, *The Icelandic Saga*. Lincoln: University of Nebraska Press, 1962. An expert in saga literature relates the origin of the sagas and explains how their frank, matter-of-fact language and style reveals the outlook of the Viking age.

Gwyn Jones, *A History of the Vikings*. Oxford, Great Britain: Oxford University Press, 1968. A complete, scholarly history of the Vikings, from their origins in the northern Germanic migrations to the death of Harald

Hardraade. Updated in 1984, the book relies extensively on contemporary accounts.

Prudence Jones and Nigel Pennick, *A History of Pagan Europe*. London: Routledge, 1995. A survey of pre-Christian societies in Europe, from Greeks and Romans to Celts, Slavs, Germans, and Vikings. A description of pagan gods and goddesses, faith, worship, and magic, and how the early Christian Church adapted these practices to the new faith.

Magnus Magnusson, *Vikings!* New York: E. P. Dutton, 1980. Adventures in the far-flung Viking world, written in an anecdotal and conversational style that gives the reader the sense of being taken on a guided tour through the surprising, little-known facets of Viking archaeology.

Eric Oxenstierna, *The Norsemen*. New York: New York Graphic Society, 1965. A richly illustrated and subjective account of the Vikings, using skaldic poetry and the sagas as a poetic background to Viking history, town life, religion, and trade.

K. R. G. Pendlesohn, *The Vikings*. New York: Windward Books, 1980. A short, subjective, and somewhat outdated general survey of Viking history.

Else Roesdahl and David M. Wilson, eds., *From Viking to Crusader: The Scandinavians and Europe, 800–1200*. New York: Rizzoli International, 1992. An encyclopedic collection of Viking art and artifacts, published in conjunction with a large traveling exhibition, "The Vikings and Europe." Along with a complete catalog of the exhibition, forty-one essays by experts and specialists in Viking studies, from "House and Home" to "Dress" to "Gold and Silver-Smithing" and "Walrus Ivory in Western Europe."

P. H. Sawyer, *The Age of the Vikings*. London: Camelot Press, 1962. A skeptical and scientific look at Viking society, using a wide range of raw archaeological data—such as coin hoards and runestone counts—to correct old myths and misconceptions about early Scandinavia.

H. G. Wells, *The Outline of History, Being a Plain History of Life and Mankind*. Garden City, NY: Garden City, 1931. One English writer's personal account of world history. The work is outdated and Eurocentric, but interesting for its stylish writing and novelistic insights into human events.

Robert Wernick, *The Vikings*. Alexandria, VA: Time-Life Books, 1979. A glossy "coffee table" book about the Vikings, with color photographs as well as contemporary line drawings illustrating Viking ships, towns, and people.

Dorothy Whitelock, ed., *The Anglo-Saxon Chronicle*. Brunswick, NJ: Rutgers University Press, 1961. One of several translations of this important contemporary document, which gives a year-by-year account of events in pre-conquest England. Well designed and extensively footnoted.

Index

giants, 76–77
godar (chiefs), 39
Gokstad ship, 82
Gotland, 20, 47
government, 34, 36, 38–40
Graham-Campbell, James
　on art, 73
　on jewelry, 71
　on longships, 25–26
　on sighting of America, 27
　on smithies, 58
Great Britain. *See* Britain
Greenland, 55–56, 59, 61
gripping beast, 72
Guthrum (Viking chief), 18–19

Hammer of Thor, 75, 77
Harald Hadrada (king of Norway), 62
Harald Sigurdsson, 30
Harold (king of Britain), 33
Harold (Viking king), 15
Harold Hardraade (Harold the Ruthless), 26, 33
Harold I Håfager (Harold Fairhair, king of Norway), 38, 39
Harold II Bluetooth (king of Denmark), 67, 84, 85
Hastings, Battle of, 21, 33
Havamal (Sayings of the High One), 50, 65–66, 69
Hebrides Islands, 14, 65
Hedeby, 45, 55, 61, 62
Heimdall, 83
History of the Vikings, A (Jones), 72
hneftafl (board game), 53
hoards, 47, 58
Horik (Danish king), 32
hospitality, 49–50
houses, 44–46, 48–49
Hrolf. *See* Rollo

Ibn al-Tartushi
　on feasts, 78
　on music, 79
Ibn Fadlan
　on appearance of Vikings, 52
　on burial customs, 80
　on punishment for crimes, 40
　on Rus traders, 61
Ibn Khurdadhbib, 19–20

Iceland
　conversion to Christianity in, 84–85
　farming in, 55
　feuds in, 41–42
　government of, 39
　sagas of, 8, 69
Ireland, 11, 14
iron, 57–58
Isle of Man, 14, 40, 65
ivory, 59

jarls (chieftains), 36–37
Jellinge style, 72
Jelling stones, 67, 72
jewelry, 20, 59, 71, 78
Jomsvikings, 32–33
Jones, Gwyn
　on defenses of towns, 44
　on gripping-beast motif, 72
Jones, Prudence, 75
Jotun, 76–77
Jul, 79, 85

karls (free peasants), 36
kennings (poetic metaphors), 68
King Harald's Saga (Sturluson), 26
kings, 37–38, 45. *See also specific kings*

Lambert, 16
Landnamabok, 69
land ownership, 36–37, 39–40
landthings (regional assemblies), 38–39
Lapps, 37, 85
"Lay of Rig, The," 37
legal system, 34, 39–42
Lindisfarne, 11–13
Loki, 75–76, 83
longships, 23, 24–26
loot, 12, 14, 16, 28

magic, 74–75
Magnusson, Gert, 57–58
Magnusson, Magnus
　on houses, 46
　on runestones and Christianity, 67
Mammen style, 72
manufacturing, 57–58, 59–60
marriages, 35, 86
Midgard, 74, 83

migrations. *See* settlements
mining, 57–58
Mjollnir, 75, 77
money. *See* coins
mounds, burial, 34, 81
music, 79

navigation, 12, 29
Neustria, 16
Niflheim, 76
Njord, 75
Nordmanni, 15
Normandy, 17–18, 65, 86
norns (goddesses), 76
Norse language
　spoken, 11, 64–65
　written
　　Romanized, 42, 68, 69
　　runes, 65–68
Norsemen, The (Oxenstierna), 40
Northmen. *See* Vikings
Northumbria, 18
Norway
　conversion to Christianity in, 84
　farming in, 55
　raids and, 28, 33
　runestones in, 65
　settlements and, 14, 30

Odin
　berserkers and, 30
　characteristics of, 74
　creation and, 74
　end of world and, 83
　magic and, 74–75
　raids and, 16, 30
　runes and, 65–66
　sayings of, 69
Olaf I Trygvasson (king of Norway), 84
Olaf Skautkonung (king of Sweden), 38
Oleg (prince of Novgorod), 19
Orkney Islands, 14, 65
Orm (Viking leader), 31
Oseberg ship, 82, 86
Othere (Norwegian chieftain), 37
Oxenstierna, Eric
　on archaeology and burial mounds, 81
　on Icelandic sagas, 8
　on importance of clans, 40
　on use of coins, 62–63

on Yule celebration, 79

paganism
    art and, 64
    burial customs of, 50, 52, 77,
      80–83
    ceremonies of, 78–79, 85
    Christian view of, 20, 22
    creation and, 69, 74
    end of world and, 83
    giants of, 76–77
    gods of, 44, 74–78
      see also specific gods
    kings and, 38
    magic and, 74–75
    redemption beliefs and, 83
peasants, 36
Pennick, Nigel, 75
personal hygiene, 52
Photius, 20
Poetica Edda, 69
poetry, 8, 68–69
polygamy, 35, 86
population, 16, 26, 43

Ragnar (Danish chief), 16
Ragnarok, 74, 83
raids
    armies and, 31, 33
    clans and, 32–33
    conversion to Christianity and,
      84
    effects of, 29
    paganism and, 76
    reasons for, 26–27
      land, 14, 16
      loot, 12, 14
    tactics of, 13, 28, 30, 31–33
    timing of, 14, 15, 27–28
    weapons used during, 30
ransom, 16–17
religion. *See* Christianity; pagan-
   ism
Ringerike style, 73
ring forts, 44
Roesdahl, Else, 22
Rollo (Danish chieftain), 17, 65,
   86
Romanesque style, 73
runestones, 35, 65–68
Rurik (Rus leader), 19
Rus, 19–21, 61
Russia, 19, 22

Sarimmer, 76
Sawyer, P. H.
    on importance of archaeology
      and coins, 9
    on Viking raids, 26–27
Scotland, 13, 14
seid (magic), 74–75
settlements, 29
    of Danes, 17, 18–19, 21, 30
    of Norwegians, 14, 30
    reasons for, 16
Shetland Islands, 14, 65
ships, 23, 40, 43
    burials and, 82
    design of, 12, 15, 24–26
Siegfried (Viking leader), 31
silver, 58, 59–60
skalds (poets), 68
slaves, 35–36, 37
Sleipnir, 76
smithies, 58, 59–60
social classes, 35–38
Sogubrot, 33
sports, 54
stallion bouts, 54
St. Clair-sur-Epte, Treaty of, 17
Steinsland, Gro
    on *blot*, 79
    on gods and giants, 77
Sturluson, Snorri
    on dragon ships, 26
    on skalds, 69–71
Sweden
    conversion to Christianity in,
      22, 84, 85–86
    farming in, 55
    iron in, 57
    runestones in, 65, 67
    trade and, 19
Swein Estridsson (king of Denmark), 62
Sweyn I Forkbeard (king of
   Denmark), 21, 38
swords, 51–52

things (assemblies), 36, 38–39
Thor, 14, 44, 75, 77, 83
Thorgeirr Ljosvetningagodi,
   84–85
thralls (slaves), 35–36, 37
Tostig (English noble), 33
towns, 43–45
toys, 53–54

trade, 43, 60
    in Britain, 11
    coins and, 61–63
    conversion to Christianity and,
      84
    Greenland and, 59, 61
    growth of, 55
    in Russia, 19
tribute, 37
Turges (Norwegian chief and
   king of Ireland), 14

Ull, 78
Urnes style, 73
Utgard, 74, 76

Valhalla, 76, 83
Valkyries, 76
Vanir, 75, 76, 77, 83
Varangian Guard, 21, 33
Viga-Glums Saga, 54
Vigrid, 83
Vikings
    appearance of, 13, 52
    end of, 21–22
    importance of, 8, 22
Vikings! (Magnusson), 67
Vikings, The (Arbman), 57
Vikings, The (Brondsted), 62
Vikings, The (Wernick), 86
Viking World, The (Graham-
   Campbell), 27
Vladimir (prince of Kiev), 22
Voluspa, 69

warfare. *See* raids
weapons, 30, 51–52, 58
Wells, H. G., 22
wergild (blood money), 42
Wernick, Robert
    on berserkers, 30
    on conversion of Rollo, 86
    on feuds, 41–42
    on Gokstad burial ship, 82
    on raids, 29, 31
Wessex, 29
William the Conqueror, 21, 33,
   42
Wilson, David M., 22
women, 33, 35

Yggdrasil, 65, 74
Yule, 79, 85

Index **95**

Picture Credits

Cover photo: Scala/Art Resource, NY
Archive Photos, 15, 25, 71, 82
Archive Photos/American Stock, 10
Corbis-Bettmann, 19, 20, 24, 27, 51, 53, 76, 81
D.Y./Art Resource, NY, 48
Christel Gerstenberg/Corbis, 32
Charles & Josette Lenars/Corbis, 73
Library of Congress, 9, 14, 26
North Wind Picture Archives, 41
Carmen Redondo/Corbis, 68
Ted Spiegel/Corbis, 45, 46, 63
Stock Montage, Inc., 13, 18, 28, 31, 35, 36, 38, 56, 70, 75, 85

Werner Forman Archive/Art Resource, NY, 58
Werner Forman Archive/National Museum, Denmark/Art Resource, NY, 59
Werner Forman Archive/National Museum of Copenhagen, Denmark/Art Resource, NY, 77
Werner Forman Archive/Statens Historiska Museet, Stockholm/Art Resource, NY, 23, 47, 60, 66
Werner Forman Archive/Universitetets Old-saksamling, Oslo/Art Resource, NY, 52
Werner Forman Archive/Viking Ship Museum, Bygdoy, Norway/Art Resources, NY, 78

About the Author

Thomas Streissguth was born in Washington, D.C., and grew up in Minnesota. After earning a B.A. in music, he traveled in Europe and worked as a teacher and book editor. He has written more than thirty books of nonfiction, including histories, biographies, and geographies, for children and young adults. He is currently working on his next project for Lucent Books, *The Transcontinental Railroad.*